"I was at the end of knowing what was wrong with me when the Lord brought Dr. Murray and his materials into my life. These things have been used by the Lord as a lifeline for me. I would recommend that every Christian read what he has written."

—N. M., South Carolina

"In a very compassionate manner, Dr. Murray helps ease the guilt that accompanies the inexpressible agony of depression. Based on Scripture, this treasure shows the depressed believer that he is not forsaken of God, is not an inferior Christian, and is not necessarily being punished for some sin. The author carefully explains the thoughts and feelings of the depressed and then offers cures. He concludes by very pointedly addressing those who care for the depressed. This is one of the most practical and encouraging books I have read on depression, and having suffered from depression myself, I have read many."

—S. L., Grand Rapids, Michigan

"I thank God for Dr. Murray's book. It has helped me immensely in learning and understanding the possible causes and cures for depression/anxiety, which have grabbed my innermost being at times in my life. The practical applications and clear writing for the layman are most helpful! This book chops away at the guilt that comes from being a Christian and depressed. I highly recommend this book. It has a place on my bookshelf to be read during those dark times of depression!"

—Dan Mayville, Amherstburg, Ontario, Canada

"When I was first diagnosed with depression, I was completely overcome by shame. I have a wonderful husband, five adorable children, and, most importantly, I have Christ. I thought then that real Christians DON'T get depressed.

"Dr. Murray's book, *Christians Get Depressed Too,* was recommended to me. As I read it, I cannot express the relief and comfort I received. For a little over a year I wondered if God had abandoned me, but after reading *Christians Get Depressed Too,* my faith was greatly strengthened, and I was reassured that God has not and never will forsake me. I thank Dr. Murray for the biblical and pastoral care in his book as well as the balanced approach he takes between the "all physical," "all spiritual," and "all mental" views concerning depression.

"During my depression, I felt as though I was drowning in the middle of the ocean, and this book was a life preserver to me. May God continue to use this book to uplift downcast spirits and glorify His name."

—JENI LUBBERS, GRAND RAPIDS, MICHIGAN

"As someone who has struggled with this darkness called depression, I have tried to make sense of this relentless foe for years. For the most part I have bought into the thinking that a Christian who deals with depression must be caught up in sin. Dr. Murray's book has brought a ray of sunshine on this dark subject. Gratefully now I have a keener awareness of the different attacks brought on by depression and how to handle them with the practical applications that Dr. Murray so clearly shows in this book. I am eternally blessed for having this helpful and smart book."

—JASON HAYES, WINDSOR, ONTARIO, CANADA

CHRISTIANS GET
DEPRESSED TOO

CHRISTIANS GET DEPRESSED TOO

Hope and Help for Depressed People

by

DAVID P. MURRAY

Reformation Heritage Books
Grand Rapids, Michigan

Reformation Heritage Books
2965 Leonard St. NE, Grand Rapids, MI 49525
616-977-0889 / Fax 616-285-3246
orders@heritagebooks.org
www.heritagebooks.org

Printed in the United States of America
12 13 14 15 16 17/10 9 8 7 6 5 4

Library of Congress Cataloging-in-Publication Data

Murray, David P.
  Christians get depressed too: hope and help for depressed people
/ David P. Murray.
     p. cm.
   ISBN 978-1-60178-100-0
  1. Depression, Mental—Religious aspects—Christianity.
2. Emotions—Religious aspects—Christianity. 3. Suffering—
Religious aspects—Christianity. 4. Depression, Mental. I. Title.
   BV4910.34.M87 2010
   248.8'625—dc22
                                        2010025745

For additional Reformed literature, both new and used, request a free book list from Reformation Heritage Books at the above regular or e-mail address.

Contents

To my lovely wife Shona.

Thank you for everything.
Yes, everything.

PREFACE

Perhaps you picked up this small book out of desperation. Perhaps, like many Christians, you are secretly suffering from mental or emotional distress—maybe depression or panic attacks—and you have tried many remedies but are growing no better, only worse. Or perhaps someone in your family is suffering in this way and you just don't know how to respond or help. Or possibly you are a pastor who feels helpless when you know that one of your beloved sheep suffers from mental distress. Whatever your reason for opening this book, I hope you will find something in these pages that will either help you in your suffering or that will help you in ministering to the suffering.

My choice of title, *Christians Get Depressed Too,* is intended to oppose and correct a very common Christian response to Christians suffering from depression: "But *Christians* don't get depressed!" How many times have you thought that, said that, or heard that? How many times have Christian pastors and counselors made this claim, or at least implied it? If it is true that

Christians don't get depressed, it must mean either that the Christian suffering from depression is not truly depressed, or he is not a true Christian. But if this notion is false, what extra and unnecessary pain and guilt are heaped upon an already darkened mind and broken heart!

This book will argue that some Christians *do* get depressed! In the first chapter we will consider *why* we should study depression. In the second we will ask, "*How* should we study depression?" Third, we will look at what depression is. Then we will look at the different approaches to helping people with depression. We will look at what the sufferer can do, what caregivers can do, and what the church can do.

Before we go on, though, perhaps you are wondering what qualifies me to write about this subject. That is a valid question, which I will answer in four ways. First, let me make clear that I am not a medical doctor. I have, however, checked all the contents with an experienced medical doctor and a Christian psychologist, both of whom have long and firsthand experience in treating many patients with depression.

Second, I was a pastor for twelve years in the northwest of Scotland, both in Wester Ross and the Outer Hebrides, areas with some of the highest rates of depression in the world. I have had multiple contacts with people who suffer from depression and also with some who have committed suicide. My motivation and methodology in writing, then, is not academic but practical. I desperately want to help sufferers and those who minister to them. That is why this book is short and simple. Depressed people cannot read hundreds of pages. They need short, simple, yet substantive instruction and advice. I hope these pages meet that need both for them and their loved ones. So you might want to view these pages as "Depression 101," or maybe, more accurately, "Depression 911." It is an emergency guide, a brief explanation of the condition, the causes, and the cures for both the sufferers and the caregivers. In the last chapter, I will recommend some books on depression that are more comprehensive and exhaustive. I've also included an appendix on the sufficiency of Scripture.

Third, I have had close and painful experience with depression, anxiety, and panic attacks among friends and some of those I love most in this world. We have been through many deep waters together, and we have arrived on the shores of God's persevering and preserving grace again. We bear the scars of battle, but we also have real-life stories to tell.

Fourth, I believe that God has given me a burden to write on this subject, a burden that I cannot ignore any longer. And I trust that with the God-given burden will come the God-given wisdom to write in such a way that will minister to God's suffering people.

ACKNOWLEDGMENTS

I'd like to thank Joel Beeke and Jay Collier of Reformation Heritage Books for publishing this book. Thanks also to Annette Gysen for her sensitive editing, to Linda den Hollander for her thoughtful typesetting, and to Derek Naves for the striking cover design.

I am especially grateful to all who have allowed me into their lives to help them through periods of depression. I have learned so much from you and your beautiful grace in the furnace of affliction.

My dear wife, Shona, has been a constant source of loving encouragement to me. Her medical expertise and spiritual counsel have balanced everything I've written.

Above all, I am thankful to God for the immense privilege of being called to serve His hurting people. May He use this book to help, heal, and wipe away their tears.

1 ⟂ The Crisis

There are many different kinds of mental and emotional suffering. The area I am particularly concerned with here is the most common—depression. As anxiety and panic attacks are also commonly associated with depression (so much so that doctors are increasingly using the term *depression-anxiety* when referring to depression), much of what I write will apply to these distressing conditions also.

But why should we study this subject at all? Here are eight reasons.

Because the Bible Speaks about It

There are numerous Bible verses that refer to the causes, consequences, and cures of depression and severe anxiety. The Bible does not address every cause and consequence. Nor does it point to every cure. But, as we shall see later, the Bible does have an important role to play in the treatment of Christians who are suffering from depression and anxiety.

The Bible never states that "Bible Character X had mental illness," or "Bible Character Y was depressed." However, it does frequently describe men and women who manifested many of the symptoms of depression and anxiety. In some cases it is not clear whether these symptoms reflect long-term mental illness or simply a temporary dip in the person's mental and emotional health, which everyone goes through from time to time. For example, symptoms of depression-anxiety can be seen in Moses (Num. 11:14), Hannah (1 Sam. 1:7, 16), and Jeremiah (Jer. 20:14–18; Lam. 3:1–6). In these cases it is difficult to say whether the symptoms reflect a depression or a dip. Martin Lloyd-Jones argues from biblical evidence that Timothy suffered from near-paralyzing anxiety.[1] A more persuasive case for a depression diagnosis can be made for Elijah (1 Kings 19:1–18), Job (Job 6:2–3, 14; 7:11), and various psalmists (Ps. 42:1–3, 9; Ps. 88). Steve Bloem, a pastor who has passed through deep and dark depressions, writes:

> The Psalms treat depression more realistically than many of today's popular books on Christianity and psychology. David and other psalmists often found themselves deeply depressed for various reasons. They did not, however, apologize for what they were feeling, nor did they confess it as

---

1. *Spiritual Depression* (London: Pickering & Inglis, 1965), 93ff.

sin. It was a legitimate part of their relationship with God. They interacted with Him through the context of their depression.[2]

Another significant verse is, "The spirit of a man will sustain his infirmity; but a wounded spirit who can bear?" (Prov. 18:14). The human spirit can help people through all kinds of bodily sickness. However, as Steve Bloem points out, "When the healing mechanism is what needs to be healed, that's a serious problem."[3]

Because It Is So Common

One in five people experiences depression, and one in ten experiences a panic attack at some stage in his life. An estimated 121 million people worldwide suffer from depression. Studies show that 5.8 percent of men and 9.5 percent of women will experience a depressive episode in any given year. Suicide, sometimes the end result of depression, is the leading cause of violent deaths worldwide, accounting for 49.1 percent of all violent deaths compared with 18.6 percent in war and 31.3 percent by homicide.[4]

It is also not uncommon among professing Christians. Indeed, these days there would appear to be an

---

2. Steve and Robyn Bloem, *Broken Minds* (Grand Rapids: Kregel, 2005), 204.

3. Ibid., 205.

4. Ibid., 54–55.

epidemic of depression, anxiety, and panic attacks among Christians—both young and old. This is partly because of the depressing state of the church and the nation. Frequently we hear discouraging news about church splits or problems and about Christians backsliding or falling into temptation. Then there is the secular and anti-Christian direction of many governments as they continue to dismantle the Judeo-Christian laws and standards that our civilization was built upon and as they attack and undermine family life. There is the relentless audio-visual misrepresentation and persecution of Christians through the print and broadcast media. To top it all, there seems to be an unceasing diet of bad news on the international stage with wars, terrorism, and natural disasters ever before us.

It is therefore little wonder that Christians react adversely and get depressed and anxious about themselves, their families, their church, and the world they live in.

Because It Impacts Our Spiritual Life

We are made up of body and soul. However, there is a third dimension that links or overlaps these two elements, which we can also view as our thoughts and feelings. When our body is sick, even with a common cold, often our spiritual life and our thinking and feeling processes are affected as well. When our spiritual life is in poor condition, our thoughts and feelings are affected, and sometimes our bodily health and functions also. It is, therefore, no surprise that when our mental and emotional health is poor and when our thinking and feeling processes go awry, there are detrimental physical and spiritual consequences. The depressed believer cannot concentrate to read or pray. As she doesn't want to meet people, she may avoid church and fellowship. She often feels God has abandoned her.

Faith, instead of being a help, can sometimes cause extra problems in dealing with depression. There is, for instance, the false guilt associated with the false conclusion that real Christians don't get depressed. There is also the oft-mistaken tendency to locate the cause of our mental suffering in our spiritual life, in our relationship with God, which also increases false guilt and feelings of worthlessness.

Because It May Be Prevented or Mitigated

Many people have a genetic predisposition to depression, perhaps traceable to their parents' genes, which increases the likelihood of suffering it themselves. However, even in these cases, knowledge of some of the other factors that may be involved in causing depression can sometimes help prevent it, or at least mitigate and shorten it.

Others, with no genetic predisposition to depression, can fall into it, often as a reaction to traumatic life events. Again, having some knowledge of mental and emotional health strategies and techniques can be especially useful in preventing, mitigating, or shortening the illness.

An additional benefit of having some knowledge about depression is that it will prevent the dangerous and damaging misunderstanding that often leads people, especially Christians, to view medication as a rejection of God and His grace rather than a provision of God and His grace.

Because It Will Open Doors of Usefulness

Increased understanding of depression will make us more sympathetic and useful to people suffering from it. If we saw someone fighting for life in the midst of a freezing blizzard, the last thing we would do is take his coat away. Such an action would be cruel and heartless and could easily lead to death. But, the Bible says, we are effectively doing the same thing if we try to help a depressed friend with superficial humor and insensitive exhortations to cheer up (Prov. 25:20).

In later chapters we will look in more detail at what friends and caregivers should say to and do for those suffering from depression and anxiety. However, the general rule is that those who listen most and speak least will be the most useful to sufferers.

Because It Is So Misunderstood

John Lockley writes: "Being depressed is bad enough in itself, but being a depressed Christian is worse.

And being a depressed Christian in a church full of people who do not understand depression is like a little taste of hell."[5]

There is a terrible stigma attached to depression. This is the result of widespread misunderstanding about its causes, its symptoms, and the cures available. Some of the misunderstanding is understandable. Unlike cancer, heart disease, or arthritis, there is no scan or test that can visibly demonstrate the existence of depression-anxiety.[6] It is a largely "invisible" disease. We want to be able to point to something and say, "There's the problem!" When we can't, we often wrongly conclude that there is no problem. Or, if we are Christians, we may often wrongly conclude that our spiritual life is the problem.

This misunderstanding is addressed in the excellent book *I'm Not Supposed to Feel Like This,* written by a Christian pastor, a Christian psychiatrist, and a Christian lecturer in psychiatry. Near the beginning of the book, the authors summarize what they do and do not believe about depression:

> What we believe: We believe that all Christians can experience worry, fear, upset and depression. We also believe that being a Christian does not

5. *A Practical Workbook for the Depressed Christian* (Bucks: Authentic Media, 1991), 14.

6. It looks like the increasing sophistication of MRI and PET scanning will make such tests possible in the near future.

prevent us or our loved ones from experiencing upsetting and challenging problems such as illness, unemployment, or relationship and other practical difficulties. ·

What we do not believe: Although at times we all choose to act in ways that are wrong and this can lead to bad consequences for us and for others, we do not see anxiety and depression as always being the result of sin; neither do we believe that mental health problems are the result of a lack of faith.[7]

It is absolutely vital for Christians to understand and accept that while depression usually has serious consequences for our spiritual life, it is not necessarily caused by problems in our spiritual life.

Because It Is a Talent to Be Invested for God

Like all affliction in the lives of Christians, depression should be viewed as a talent (Matt. 25:14–30) that can be invested in such a way that it brings benefit to us and others as well as glory to God. Christian psychologist James Dobson observed, "Nothing is wasted in God's economy." That "nothing" includes depression.

Mind over Mood, while not written from a Christian perspective, illustrates the possible benefits of depression:

---

7. Chris Williams, Paul Richards, Ingrid Whitton, *I'm Not Supposed to Feel Like This* (London: Hodder & Stoughton, 2002), 10.

An oyster creates a pearl out of a grain of sand. The grain of sand is an irritant to the oyster. In response to the discomfort, the oyster creates a smooth, protective coating that encases the sand and provides relief. The result is a beautiful pearl. For an oyster, an irritant becomes the seed for something new. Similarly, *Mind over Mood will* help you develop something valuable from your current discomfort. The skills taught in this book will help you feel better and will continue to have value in your life long after your original problems are gone.[8]

God often uses broken people. In *Passion and Purity,* Elisabeth Elliot quotes Ruth Stull of Peru: "If my life is broken when given to Jesus, it is because pieces will feed a multitude, while a loaf will satisfy only a little lad (39)."

Because We Can All Improve Our Mental and Emotional Health

Most Christians try to take preventative (and curative) measures to enjoy a good, healthy physical and spiritual life. However, there is less consciousness of the similar effort required to maintain or recover mental health. There is much less awareness of the biblical strategies and proven techniques that can be

---

8. Dennis Greenberger and Christine Padesky, *Mind over Mood* (New York: Guilford, 1995), 1.

used to achieve good mental and emotional health, with beneficial side effects for our bodies and souls.

I have never been diagnosed with any kind of mental illness. However, like most people, and especially like most pastors, I have had low points in my life, times of mild to moderate depression and anxiety. Sometimes this was brought on by bodily pain and illness and sometimes by my thinking processes going wrong. What I now know about improving and maintaining mental and emotional health and what I hope to communicate in the following chapters would have greatly helped me in these low periods. What I have learned is helping me on a daily basis to overcome disappointment and handle stressful situations without my mental and emotional health suffering as much as before.

As I look around me, and especially as I look around the church, I can see many people who have not been diagnosed with depression and who are not disabled by it, but who are experiencing long-term, low-level depression-anxiety, which is having its own side effect on their bodily health and spiritual lives. It would not be too difficult for them to learn some sound strategies and techniques that will improve mental health and, consequently, their bodily and spiritual health. Some of these are covered in this book.

In the next chapter, we will consider the attitude and spirit in which we should study depression.

2 | THE COMPLEXITY

We began by considering eight reasons *why* the Christian should study depression. Now we will look at *how* the Christian should study depression—with what attitude and in what spirit the subject should be approached. There are two principles that should condition all our thoughts and the expression of them in studying depression.

Avoid Dogmatism and Seek Humility

First, let there be an absence of dogmatism. Where the Word of God is dogmatic, the preacher must be dogmatic. He must clearly and boldly declare God's Word with all authority. He must have no hesitation or equivocation. He must not make mere suggestions or proposals. He must pronounce, "Thus says the Lord."

Unfortunately, Christian preachers and writers have often taken a dogmatic attitude into areas where the Word of God is not dogmatic. One such area is depression. In researching this subject, I have been frequently shocked by the almost *ex cathedra* infallibility assumed by Christian writers and speakers when writing or speaking about mental and emotional suffering. This dangerous dogmatism often reflects personal prejudices and experiences rather than the principles of God's Word.

It must be admitted that confident, sweeping dogmatic certainty appeals to the writer and reader, the preacher and hearer, who crave simplicity in a confusing world. However, it is highly damaging in this complex area of depression, which requires careful, balanced, and sensitive thinking, writing, and speaking.

When we look back on the treatments that used to be offered for bodily diseases, we shudder with horror at the frequently crude and unsuitable advice and potions that were confidently given to patients. With advances in medical research, such advice and medicines now look ridiculous. It is very likely that in the future, with increased research into depression and also increased understanding of the Bible's teaching, much of the current confident certainty, which presently masquerades as biblical or medical expertise, will also look ridiculous, cruel, and even horrifying.

In our study of and in our contact with those suffering from depression, let's avoid unfounded and unwarranted dogmatism. And let's study, listen, and speak with humility and an awareness of our own ignorance and insufficiency when faced with the complex and often mysterious causes and consequences of depression.

Avoid Extremes and Seek Balance

There are three simplistic extremes that we should avoid when considering the cause of depression: first, that it is all physical; second, that it is all spiritual; third, that it is all mental. Let's examine these three positions.

The cause is all physical

For many years the foundational presupposition behind the largely drug-driven solutions offered by many doctors and psychiatrists has been that depression has purely physical causes (chemical imbalances in the brain). And, if the presupposition of a physical cause is correct (chemical deficiency), then the prescription of antidepressants (chemical correction) is a logical conclusion. This is often called the medical model, or the drug-treatment model.

There is much scientific evidence to support the drug-treatment model. Studies have demonstrated that the brains of many depressed patients have a different chemistry and circuitry compared to people with good mental and emotional health. To put it simply, the brain needs chemicals to move our thoughts through. When these chemicals are depleted, as they often are in cases of depression, then the whole process slows down, or even stops, in certain areas.

Obviously the drug-treatment model, or the all-physical model, for depression is supported by those who wish to deny the existence of a non-physical, or spiritual, element to human beings. However, there are Christians who also take the drug-treatment model approach. An example of this is found in the book *Broken Minds* by Steve and Robyn Bloem. Steve is a Christian pastor who has struggled with serious depression throughout his ministry. His book, co-written with his wife, is focused on endogenous depression (depressions that are biological or organic in origin) and gives a deeply moving account of his life-threatening battle with mental illness. There is no Christian book I know of that gives such an honest and hard-hitting insight into the pain and distress that the depressed and their families have to endure. If you wish to increase your sympathy and compassion for sufferers and their loved ones, then this heart-rending book is for you.

However, the book's greater usefulness is somewhat limited by its focus on the drug-treatment model approach to causes and cures. As we have said, there is unquestionably a physical element to most depressions, often requiring medication. And in Steve Bloem's case, there would appear to have been a large and serious physical problem that required necessary and life-saving medication. However, it is too big a step to move from this to proposing the drug-treatment model as the preferred model in almost every case and medication as the preferred solution in almost every case. In this complex area, it is presumptuous to view one's own experience as the norm for everyone else.

In some ways, the Bloems' "almost always physical causes" position is understandable. For far too long, Christian writers and speakers in this area have been overly influenced by Jay Adams's extreme position of "almost always spiritual" in both causes and cures (a discussion of this view follows). However, we must not overreact to one unhelpful extreme by adopting another.

The cause is all spiritual

This extreme position takes two forms. We will look at the first briefly and then look in more detail at the second. Third, we will consider the situations when depression does have a sole spiritual cause.

• *Depression is caused by demonic possession and requires exorcism.*

This idea is associated with some Pentecostal and charismatic churches that place a large emphasis on spiritual warfare. The spiritual warfare movement takes the view that depression (just like alcoholism and immorality) is usually due to either demonic oppression or possession. The "treatment," therefore, is to effect "deliverance" from or expulsion of these demons.

We must allow for the possibility that mental distress can be, on rare occasions, caused by demon possession.

However, as we have already highlighted, there is credible scientific evidence that connects mental suffering with physical causes, a fact confirmed by the success of medications in relieving some of the symptoms.

We can only hope that the dogmatic views and practices of the spiritual warfare movement will eventually be swept away by the increased knowledge of medical research, just like advances in research and increased education of the public eventually swept away the once common view that epilepsy was caused by demons.

• *Depression is caused by sin; therefore, rebuke, repentance, and confession are required.*

This idea is widespread in the evangelical church, largely as a result of the writings of Jay Adams's[1] nouthetic counseling movement and of those who have followed him in the modern biblical counseling movement. I will summarize Adams's approach and then highlight the strengths and weaknesses of his reasoning. Next I will consider whether the modern biblical counseling movement's attempts to nuance and refine Adams's approach have been successful.

---

1. Jay E. Adams (b. January 30, 1929) is an American Reformed Christian author who is mostly known for his book *Competent to Counsel*. See also The Institute for Nouthetic Studies: www.nouthetic.org.

The Nouthetic Counseling Movement. Like the Bloems, Jay Adams founds his approach on his own personal experience of mental illness—in his case, as he encountered it at two treatment centers in Illinois. He summarized his experience-based conclusion as follows: "Apart from those who had organic problems like brain damage, the people I met in the two institutions in Illinois were there because of *their own failure to meet life's problems* [italics added]. To put it simply, they were there because of their unforgiven and unaltered sinful behavior."[2]

On the basis of this he argues in another place: "The hope for the depressed persons, as elsewhere, lies in this: the depression is the result of the counselee's sin."[3]

If this diagnosis is correct, then we would expect the logical prescription to be rebuke and repentance or counseling with a view to conviction and conversion, and that is exactly what we find in Adams's writings. He describes his counseling method as nouthetic counseling. The word *nouthetic* is from the Greek New Testament noun *nouthesia* and verb *noutheteō,* meaning to admonish, correct, or instruct (Rom. 15:14).

---

2. *Competent to Counsel* (Grand Rapids: Zondervan, 1970), xvi.

3. *Christian Counselor Manual* (Grand Rapids: Zondervan, 1973), 378.

Following logically from Adams's belief that bad feelings are the result of bad actions is the usual nouthetic remedy: "If you do right, you feel right." If you get depressed because of sinful behavior, then, obviously, you get better by righteous behavior.

Strengths. Adams was reacting against the humanistic view that explained sinful addictions like alcoholism as sickness or that blamed immoral behavior on one's genes or that tried to remove people's guilt feelings by encouraging them to deny personal responsibility for their actions and simply accept themselves as they are. Adams's emphasis on the need to accept personal responsibility in these situations was necessary.

He also was right to expose the over-prescription of psychiatric drugs and to demand that counseling actually deal with problematic and unbiblical behavior, rather than simply make people feel better in their sin.

In addition, though he has gone too far in saying that depression is almost always spiritual, Adams has shown the need to address the spiritual dimension of mental and emotional suffering. In doing so, he restored the Bible's central role in counseling and secured the role of Christian pastors and counselors in treatments.

Adams's approach is especially useful in situations where the problem is everyday mood swings and simply feeling down. There are times in our lives when, often in response to difficult personal situations, we allow ourselves to wallow in hopeless self-pity and slip into blaming everybody else for our problems. At such times nouthetic counseling is exactly what we need. We need to be confronted with the sinfulness of our reactions and encouraged to get on with our daily duties and responsibilities.

Finally, though we may disagree with Adams's argument that depression is almost always caused by sin, we must accept that sometimes, even in depressions not caused by sinful conduct (e.g., as a result of thyroid malfunctions), people can adopt unhelpful attitudes and sinful behavior patterns, which should be sympathetically addressed and corrected.

Weaknesses. While Adams is to be commended for giving an important place to personal responsibility, he errs in placing all responsibility on the depressed patient. Adams fails to appreciate the significant difference in kind between bad moods or short-term depressions of spirit, which are sometimes sinful and to be repented of, and the deeper kinds of depression, which often have far more complex causes than the sinful choices of individuals. When comparing feeling down with depression, Adams says, "This movement from *down* (not depression) to *down and out* (depression) occurs whenever one handles down feelings sinfully (thus incurring guilt and more guilt feelings), by following them rather than his responsibilities before God."[4]

To put all the blame for depression on the individual is wrong, damaging, and dangerous, as it can only increase feelings of guilt and worthlessness. Such mistaken views have been around for a long time. Almost 150 years ago, the depressed Charles Spurgeon observed,

> It is all very well for those who are in robust health and full of spirits to blame those whose lives are sicklied or covered with the pale cast of melancholy, but the [malady] is as real as a gaping wound, and all the more hard to bear because it lies so much in the region of the soul that to the inexperienced it appears to be a mere matter of fancy and diseased imagination. Reader, never ridicule the nervous and hypochondriacal, their pain is real; though much of the [malady] lies in the imagination [thought-processes] it is not imaginary.[5]

While Adams did address sinful behavior (unlike secular counselors), he has been criticized for not going much beyond the external. His remedy of "do right and you will feel right" fails to address heart idolatry

---

4. *What about Nouthetic Counseling?* (Grand Rapids: Baker, 1977), 4n7.

5. *The Treasury of David,* 3 vols. (Newark, Del.: Cornerstone, 1869), 2.132.

and also the faulty thought processes that may have contributed to or may have even caused the depression (ten faulty thought processes will be discussed in the next chapter). Such superficial behaviorist solutions will usually fail in the long term.

For a moment, though, let's allow that Adams's diagnosis is correct in some situations. Let's imagine a person who has major depression as a result of his sinful handling of down feelings or of his sinful reactions to difficult life events. A side effect of this downward spiral is that vital brain chemicals, such as serotonin, are now depleted, and his thought circuits are malfunctioning. He is at the bottom of the black hole of depression. He cannot do anything, and he can hardly think. The last thing he needs is a preacher telling him to repent and shouting down the hole, "Do right and you will feel right!" Or, "Repent of your idolatry!" He needs someone to shine a light and throw down a rope. Medicine can play this role. It can restore the chemicals and circuits required to help a person think. And then, repentance can take place. We would do the same even for a person who accidentally shoots himself with a gun. We would get him to the hospital and give him whatever medical treatment he needs before addressing any sinful carelessness that may have caused the problem.

As noted, the nouthetic counseling movement grew out of a frustration at the way in which secular doctors and psychiatrists squeezed Christian pastors and counselors out of any role in the treatment of mental illness. However, in the valiant and commendable attempt to secure a much-needed place for Christian pastors and counselors in the treatment of mental illness, the nouthetic counseling movement has often gone to the opposite extreme in attempting to exclude doctors, psychologists, and psychiatrists from the treatment process. In both cases the sufferer is the one who loses out.

I realize that our responses to helping people with problems are often determined by our previous experiences. And it may be that, like Adams, we have had the painful experience of trying to deal with depressed people who will not accept responsibility for their sin (I certainly have). However, I believe we have to fight against making that experience our default starting point in dealing with depressed people. It might be our ending point, but it should not be our starting point.

Before I leave this brief section on Jay Adams, I do want to say that while many have criticized Adams for being harsh and unsympathetic, those who know him have found him to be a kind and loving Christian man. Perhaps the problem lies more in how people have put his presuppositions into practice.

The Modern Biblical Counseling Movement. The modern biblical counseling movement is best represented by the personnel and ministry of CCEF (Christian Counseling and Education Foundation).

The Christian church has much reason to thank God for the wonderful work done by CCEF's past and present faculty. By God's grace, they have continued Adams's pioneering reformation of Christian counseling practice. They have responded to some of the criticisms of Adams by presenting a more nuanced and sympathetic approach to counseling Christians with depression and other mental and emotional problems. CCEF books have been a blessing to me personally, and I use the foundation's materials extensively in the counseling courses I teach at Puritan Reformed Theological Seminary. I dread to think what a mess Christian counseling might be in today without the courageous and wise leadership of the biblical counseling movement.

My main concern with the nouthetic counseling movement is its assumption that behind almost every episode of depression is personal sin. Regrettably, the modern biblical counseling movement still uses language that supports this conclusion. Admittedly, they have changed the focus in their search for the counselee's sin from Adams's external behaviorism to the more biblical and spiritual issues of heart-idolatry. However, in most cases, the search for sin remains their default starting position; the problem is sin, the cure is repentance. Ed Welch's *Blame It on the Brain?* is considerably more sensitive and discriminating.

Given the historical context of the nouthetic counseling movement's emphases, we might hope that the leaders of the modern biblical counseling movement would strive to use consistently clear and unambiguous language when speaking or writing about the causes and cures of depression. In some places they do concede that depression is not always caused by sin, and even allow for medication in certain cases. However, too often, language is still used that would lead most readers or hearers to think that all depression is caused by personal sin, that medication is always a sinful response to depression (treating only superficial symptoms), and that repentance of heart-idolatry is always the cure.[6]

We would never take this view (sinful cause/spiritual solution) when counseling people with cancer, strokes, broken legs, diabetes, or Alzheimer's. As Reformed Christians, our default position is that these physical problems are most likely the result of living as fallen creatures in a fallen world. Why should our default position with brain problems be any different? Are we saying that the brain, the most complex organ

---

6. It is potentially misleading to associate chemical or hormonal explanations of depression with those that are always sinful. See David Powlison, *Seeing with New Eyes* (Philipsburg, N.J.: P&R, 2003), 125–26, 129–30. It is also potentially harmful when, without careful qualification, taking medication for depression is associated with responses that are always sinful. See David Powlison, *Seeing with New Eyes*, 76–77, 129–30. Also, David Powlison, *Speaking Truth in Love*, (Glenside, Pa.: Vantage Point, 2005) 41, 112–13, 154.

in our body, is somehow exempt from the effects of the Fall? My skin is broken down by psoriasis, my eyes are broken down with shortsightedness, my nose is broken down with rhinitis, my joints are sometimes broken with arthritis, my bowel has required two operations, my legs are broken down with varicose veins, my body is covered with dangerous moles (two of which have been removed), but I am actually very healthy! I do not believe any of these ailments are the result of personal sin but simply either the consequences of being a fallen creature living in a fallen world or of inheriting genes from my mother and father who have also had similar health issues. Why then should we always have to conclude that brain disorders are the result of personal sin? As the authors of *I'm Not Supposed to Feel Like This* explain: "Being a Christian does not inoculate us from the possibility of experiencing anxiety or depression; many Christians have experienced quite severe depressive illnesses. This is true in the same way that being a Christian does not prevent you from becoming ill or falling victim to crime or assault."[7]

Am I saying that brain illness is never caused by personal sin? No, not at all! Just as heart disease can be caused by abusing the body with smoking or alcohol, just as some diabetes can be caused by gluttony,

---

7. Chris Williams, Paul Richards, Ingrid Whitton (London: Hodder & Stoughton, 2002), 33.

just as a broken leg can be caused by pushing the body beyond God-given limitations, so brain illness can be caused by personal sin. However, our default position in understanding how the brain can experience problems should be no different from that of understanding these other physical problems.

• *Depression can sometimes be caused by sin.*

When a Christian becomes depressed, the first conclusion he usually jumps to is that the cause is spiritual, that his relationship with God, or poverty of it, is all to blame. While most depressed Christians will feel that their relationship with God is all wrong and all to blame, this overly self-critical feeling is usually one of the fruits of depression and, therefore, is often wrong. It is important for Christians in such situations to doubt, question, and even challenge the accuracy of their feelings, as they usually do not reflect the facts.

Having said that, however, it is important to acknowledge the possibility of a primarily spiritual cause to some depressions. The psalms of lament describe the depressed feelings of the psalmists, which were usually no fault of their own. However, we do also have Psalms 32 and 51, which clearly link the traumatic physical, emotional, and mental symptoms of depression with David's sins of murder and adultery.

In a later chapter I will examine how to decide if depression has spiritual causes or simply spiritual consequences. However, I agree with the general stance taken by the authors of *I'm Not Supposed to Feel Like This,* that we should, in general, reassure Christians suffering from depression that most often their damaged spiritual relationships and feelings are not the cause of their depression, but the consequence of it. That is, we should assume the same default position with someone suffering from depression as with someone who has shortsightedness, diabetes, heart disease, or a broken leg. We should assume the depression is a result of living as a fallen creature in a fallen world rather than assume that the person has caused his suffering by his personal sin. If we are wrong, in the course of counseling we will soon find out and wisely adopt a different approach.

The cause is all mental ("in the mind")

"It's all in the mind" can mean two different things. Some people who use this expression may be correctly identifying the seat of a depression—the chemical imbalances in the brain. However, most people who use it are incorrectly alleging that the depression is a fiction, a delusion, something made up. Usually implicit in this view, and sometimes explicit, is the idea that the depressed person is someone with a weak and fragile mind.

Charles Spurgeon, who suffered from frequent deep depression and anxiety and who could hardly be accused of mental weakness, addressed this fallacy in the quote we looked at previously: "Reader, never ridicule the nervous and hypochondriacal, their pain is real; though much of the [malady] lies in the imagination [thought-processes] it is not imaginary."[8]

Depression afflicts the strong and the weak, the clever and the simple, those with a happy temperament and those of a melancholy temperament. Never was the caution so much needed, "Let him that thinketh he standeth take heed lest he fall" (1 Cor. 10:12).

We need to recognize the exceeding complexity of depression and resist the temptation to propose and accept simple analyses and solutions. Just as no two hearts are identically diseased, and just as no two cancers are the same, no two depressions are the same in cause, symptoms, depth, duration, and cure. Therefore, we must avoid making our own experience the norm for others.

The body, the soul, and the thoughts and feelings are extremely complicated entities. The interrelation of the physical, the spiritual, and the mental and emotional is even more complicated. Unravelling the sequence of what went wrong in a depressed person's brain, soul, or thoughts is often a humanly impossible task. Analysis of the mental, emotional, physical, and spiritual contributions to the situation is equally difficult. Dr. Martyn Lloyd-Jones wrote, "Christians don't

---

8. *The Treasury of David*, 3 vols. (Newark, DE: Cornerstone, 1869), 2.132.

understand how physical, psychological, and spiritual realms interrelate because Satan muddies the boundaries. Many of our troubles are caused because we think a problem is spiritual when it is physical or we think a problem is physical when it is emotional or spiritual."[9]

The Puritans were incomparable experts in soul care. But even they were well aware of the possibility of depression being caused by brain malfunction. William Perkins spent hours counseling people every week and distinguished between melancholy with a physical cause requiring medicine, and conviction of sin, which had a spiritual cause and required the blood of Christ: "Sorrow, that comes by melancholy ariseth only of that humour [sickness] annoying the bodies: but this other sorrow, ariseth of a man's sins, for which his conscience accuses him. Melancholy may be cured by physicke [medicine]: this sorrow cannot be cured by anything but the blood of Christ.[10]

Jonathan Edwards, who had seen depression in his mother's family, quotes appreciatively the insight and counsel of Perkins:

---

9. *The Christian Warfare* (Grand Rapids: Baker, 1976), 206–8. See all of chapter 15 in *The Christian Warfare*, "Physical, Psychological, Spiritual."

10. *William Perkins 1558–1602: English Puritanist. His Pioneer Works on Casuistry: "A Discourse of Conscience" and "The Whole Treatise of Cases of Conscience,"* ed. Thomas C. Merrill (Nieuwkoop: B. De Graaf, 1966), 39–40.

> The famous Mr. Perkins distinguishes between those sorrows that come through convictions of conscience, and melancholic passions arising only from mere imagination, strongly conceived in the brain; which, he says, "usually come on a sudden, like lightning into a house."[11]

Edwards also connected physical disease of the brain with mental suffering and depression in his *Treatise on Religious Affections*.[12]

All this reminds us that the prescription of solutions is often a matter that takes much time, and even trial and error. There are usually no quick fixes. For Christians there will often need to be a balance between medicines for the brain, rest for the body, counsel for the mind, and spiritual encouragement for the soul. Recovery will usually take patient perseverance over a period of many months, and in some cases, even years.

Therefore, great care is required in coming to conclusions about our own condition or that of others. It is important to remember the two main principles that govern our understanding of depression: Avoid dogmatism and seek humility. Avoid extremes and seek balance.

---

11. *Works of Jonathan Edwards [WJE]. Volume 2, A Treatise Concerning Religious Affections*, ed. John E. Smith (New Haven: Yale University Press, 1959), 157 (accessed December 10, 2009).

12. WJE, 2:216; 2:290.

3 | THE CONDITION

We began with eight reasons *why* we should study depression and with two principles to govern *how* we should study depression. We also examined three extreme positions some take regarding the cause of depression: all physical, all spiritual, or all mental (or psychological). We concluded that it was vital to resist the extremes and instead to recognize the causes of depression to be complex and varied. Dr. Martyn Lloyd-Jones underlined the importance of this point:

> Many Christian people, in fact, are in utter ignorance concerning this realm where the borderlines between the physical, psychological and spiritual meet. Frequently I have found that such [church] leaders had treated those whose trouble was obviously mainly physical or psychological, in a purely spiritual manner; and if you do so, you not only don't help. You aggravate the problem.[1]

---

1. *The Christian Warfare* (Grand Rapids: Baker, 1976), 206–208.

Having laid this groundwork, we can now consider this question: what is depression? There are two reasons we should be concerned about getting a right answer to this question. The first is physical and the second is spiritual.

The physical reason is that only by knowing the symptoms can I know if others or I are suffering from depression and then seek appropriate help. Many people suffer varying degrees of depression without knowing it because they do not recognize the symptoms. Sadly, they often go years without getting help that is readily available and that would transform their lives.

The spiritual reason, and the one I am most concerned about, is that many who have the symptoms of depression, without identifying them as such, reason, "If I have these thoughts and feelings, I cannot be a Christian!" My aim in this chapter is not only to outline the symptoms of depression, but also to show from Scripture that such symptoms are not only compatible with being a Christian but are also found in some of the most eminent Bible characters.

We will answer the question "What is depression?" by looking at how it is related to and reflected in five areas of our lives: our life situation, our thoughts, our feelings, our bodies, and our behavior. Before we do so, however, we must state three caveats. First, these five areas are all interrelated. We cannot separate our thoughts from our feelings or our feelings from our behavior. What we think affects how we feel. What we think and feel affects our physical health. Our thoughts, feelings, and physical health affect what we do. To illustrate how connected we are, just think of the last time you had the flu and how this impacted your feelings, concentration, mental alertness, physical abilities, and prayer life.

Second, the sequence in which we discuss these areas is not necessarily the chronological order in which the symptoms of depression always manifest themselves.

Third, we will focus most of our attention on our thoughts, as false thought patterns are often the biggest contributor to depression and also because it is an area where, with God's grace, we can most help ourselves.

Life Situation

Life in this world is full of ups and downs. Our providence can change rapidly from smooth and happy to rough and upsetting. It is important to recognize how providential changes (such as bereavement, loss of job, family difficulties, relationship problems, and lack of money) can seriously damage our mental and emotional health. A person may feel down and yet never link these feelings with such life events. Therefore, one of the first steps in treating depression is to take time to examine our lives and, with God's help, to trace our present depressed thoughts and feelings to events in our lives.

This can be a painful process of self-discovery. Although we are frail and weak creatures, we like to think that we can cope with everything that life throws at us. We are often reluctant to link our depressed thoughts or anxiety to life situations because such a link exposes our weakness and frailty. As a result, there is often a desperate search for a purely physical cause (such as a virus) for our lack of well-being, because that will enable us to keep viewing ourselves as "mentally strong."

This is not to deny that there are usually, to one degree or another, physical factors involved in causing depression, as I explained in the previous chapter. Indeed, in some people, there is very likely an inherited genetic tendency to depression. However, there is almost always a providential trigger involved to some degree. Just because we coped with great stresses at some time in our lives does not guarantee that we will cope with lesser stresses at other points in our lives. We age, our hormones and brain chemistry change, and our responsibilities increase as marriage and children come along. Sometimes an adverse reaction to life events will be delayed, even for some years.

Consequently, we often need an objective view of our lives. Independent people such as a doctor, a counselor, or a pastor can help us look at our lives more objectively. Often, when we are helped to review our lives, we begin to see the real and significant effects our problems or difficulties have had on us and the extent to which they may have contributed to our depression or anxiety. The Puritan, Richard Baxter, spoke similarly about the need to seek the counsel of others:

> Consider that it should be easy for you in your confounding, troubling thoughts, to perceive that your understandings are not now so sound and strong as other men's; and therefore be not willful and self-conceited, and think not that your thoughts are righter than theirs, but believe wiser men, and be ruled by them.[2]

Thoughts

Perhaps the most obvious symptoms of depression are the depressed person's unhelpful thought patterns, which tend to distort his view of reality in a false and negative way, adding to his depression or anxiety. As the writers of *Mind over Mood* put it, "Our *perception* of an event or experience powerfully affects our emotional, behavioral, and physiological responses to it." Or, as the Bible puts it: "As [a man] thinketh in his heart, so is he" (Prov. 23:7).

While we often cannot change the providences we are passing through, we can change the way we think

---

2. "The Cure of Melancholy and Overmuch Sorrow," in *The Practical Works of Rev. Richard Baxter,* 4 vols. (London: George Virtue, 1838), 4:932.

about them so we can have a more accurate and positive view of our lives, thereby lifting our spirits.

I will focus on ten false thought patterns that reflect, but also contribute to, the symptoms of depression. I will summarize each thought habit and look at three examples of each: one from ordinary life, another from our spiritual life, and another from the Bible. The biblical examples are not necessarily depressed people, but they are examples of the false thought patterns often present in a depressed person.

It is important to see how our depressed thought patterns affect our ordinary life and even more important to see how that is then carried into our spiritual life. It is usually that order in which our thoughts are transferred—false thinking in ordinary life is eventually transferred into our spiritual life.

False extremes[3]

This is a tendency to evaluate personal qualities in extreme, black-and-white categories; shades of gray do not exist. This is sometimes called all-or-nothing thinking.

---

3. Most of these thought patterns are identified in most books that deal with depression. The books I found most helpful are *I'm Not Supposed to Feel Like This* (London: Hodder & Stoughton, 2002) and *Feeling Good* (New York: Avon Books, 1999).

Life example: You make one mistake in cooking a meal and conclude you are a total disaster.

Spiritual example: You have a sinful thought in prayer and conclude that you are an apostate.

Biblical example: Despite most of his life being characterized by God's blessing and prosperity, when Job passed through a time of suffering, he decided he must be an enemy of God (Job 13:24; 33:10).

False generalization

This happens when, after experiencing one unpleasant event, we conclude that the same thing will happen to us again and again.

Life example: If a young man's feelings for a young woman are rebuffed, he concludes that this will always happen to him and that he will never marry any woman.

Spiritual example: When you try to witness to someone, you are mocked, and you conclude that this will always happen to you and that you will never win a soul for Christ.

Biblical example: At a low point in his own life, Jacob deduced that because Joseph was dead and Simeon was captive in Egypt that Benjamin would also be taken from him

(Gen. 42:36). "All these things are against me," he generalized.

False filter

When we are depressed, we tend to pick out the negative in every situation and think about it alone, to the exclusion of everything else. We filter out anything positive and decide everything is negative.

Life example: You get ninety percent on an exam, but all you can think about is the ten percent you got wrong.

Spiritual example: You heard something in a sermon you did not like or agree with and went home thinking and talking only about that part of the service.

Biblical example: Despite having just seen God's mighty and miraculous intervention on Mount Carmel, Elijah filtered out all the positives and focused only on the continued opposition of Ahab and Jezebel (1 Kings 19:10).

False transformation

Another aspect of depression is that we transform neutral or positive experiences into negative ones. The depressed person doesn't ignore positive experiences; rather, she disqualifies them or turns them into their opposite.

Life example: If someone compliments you, you conclude that the person is just being hypocritical or that he or she is trying to get something from you.

Spiritual example: When you receive a blessing from a verse or a sermon, you decide that it is just the devil trying to deceive you.

Biblical example: Jonah saw many Ninevites repent in response to his preaching. But in-- stead of rejoicing in this positive experience, his mood slumped so low that he angrily asked God to take away his life (Jonah 4:3–4).

False mind reading

We may think that we can tell what someone is think- ing about us, that the person hates us or views us as stupid. But such negative conclusions usually are not supported by the facts.

Life example: A friend may pass you without stopping to talk because, unknown to you, he is late for a meeting. But you conclude that he no longer likes you.

Spiritual example: Someone who used to talk to you at church now passes you with hardly a word, so you decide that you have fallen out of her favor. But, unknown to you, the person's marriage is in deep trouble, and she is too embarrassed to risk talking to anyone.

Biblical example: The psalmist one day concluded that all men were liars. On reflection, he admitted that this judgment was overly hasty (Ps. 116:11).

False fortune telling

This occurs when we feel so strongly that things will turn out badly that our feelings-based prediction seems to become an already established fact. We expect catastrophe, and the expectation itself produces hopelessness and helplessness.

Life example: You feel sure that you will always be depressed and will never be better again. This is despite the evidence that almost everybody eventually recovers.

Spiritual example: You are convinced that you will never be able to pray in public. Again, this is despite the evidence that, though difficult at first, with practice almost everybody manages it.

Biblical example: Anticipating the opposition that Jesus would face in Bethany, Thomas falsely predicted not only his own death there but also that of the Lord and the other disciples (John 11:16).

False lens

This is when we view our fears, errors, or mistakes through a magnifying glass and deduce catastrophic consequences. Everything then is out of proportion.

Life example: When you make a mistake at work, you conclude, "I'm going to be fired!"

Spiritual example: Despite having received forgiveness from God, you focus on your sins from the distant past in a way that leads to continued feelings of guilt, self-condemnation, and fear of punishment.

Biblical example: When Peter sinfully denied the Lord, he not only wept bitterly but decided that since his mistake was so spiritually catastrophic, there was no alternative but to forget about preaching Christ and go back to catching fish (John 21:3).

The other side of this is that while you maximize your faults with a magnifying glass, you also tend to look through the binoculars the wrong way when it comes to your assets—and minimize them.

False feelings-based reasoning

People suffering from depression tend to take their emotions as the truth. They let their feelings determine the facts.

Life example: You feel useless and conclude that you are useless.

Spiritual example: You feel unforgiven and conclude you are unforgiven. You feel cut off from God and conclude that you are cut off from God.

Biblical example: At one of his low points, David felt and hastily concluded that he was cut off from God. "I said in my haste, I am cut off from before thine eyes" (Ps. 31:22).

False "shoulds"

Our lives may be dominated by "shoulds" or "oughts," applied to ourselves or others. This heaps pressure on us and others to reach certain unattainable standards and causes frustration and resentment when others or we fail.

Life example: The busy mother who tries to keep her house as tidy and orderly as if there were no children is putting herself under undue pressure to reach unattainable standards.

Spiritual example: The conscientious Christian who feels that despite being responsible for taking care of her household, preparing meals and raising children, she ought also to be at every prayer meeting, worship service, and Bible study and should also serve on several church committees, prepare meals for needy church members, read good books, and always feel close to God.

Biblical example: Martha felt deep frustration that Mary was not fulfilling what she felt were her obligations and complained bitterly about it (Luke 10:40–42).

False responsibility

This is when we assume responsibility and blame ourselves for a negative outcome, even when there is no basis for this.

Life example: When your child does not get excellent grades you conclude that you are an awful mother. The real reason may be instead that your child has a poor teacher or that the child does not have academic gifts.

Spiritual example: When your child turns against the Lord and turns his back on the church, you assume that, despite doing everything you humanly could to bring him up for the Lord, it is all your fault.

Biblical example: Moses felt responsible for the negative reactions of Israel to God's providence and was so cast down about this that he prayed for death (Num. 11:14–15).

Important Points to Remember

1. False thinking patterns *are* compatible with being a Christian.

2. False thought patterns will have a detrimental effect on our feelings, our bodies, our behavior, and our souls, usually in that order.

3. One of the first steps in getting better is recognizing these false thinking patterns, which do not reflect reality.

4. While we can do little, if anything, to change our providence (our life situation), we can change the false way we may think about our providence.

Feelings

Obviously, these unhelpful thought patterns are going to give you unhelpful emotions and feelings. If you are always thinking about problems and negatives or imagine the future is hopeless or think everyone hates you, you are going to feel down very quickly. Your *feelings* about ordinary life and your spiritual life are going to reflect what you *think* in each arena (Prov. 23:7).

Here, I will briefly look at some of the emotional symptoms of depression. And, as in the area of our thoughts, let us honestly examine the area of our feelings in order to consider whether our emotions are related to a depressive tendency or illness. Also, as with the area of our thoughts, in this area of feelings I will highlight biblical examples of true believers experiencing such emotions in order to show that such feelings are compatible with being a true believer.

Do you feel overwhelming sadness?

Everyone feels sad from time to time, but depression-related sadness is overwhelming and long-term. It often results in tearfulness and prolonged bouts of unstoppable sobbing. Perhaps nothing gives you any pleasure anymore, even the things you used to enjoy most. Perhaps all you can think about are sins you committed and mistakes you made.

Biblical examples: Job (Job 3:20; 6:2–3; 16:6, 16); David (Ps. 42:3, 7).

Do you feel angry with God or others?

A common characteristic of depression, especially in men, is a deep-seated and often irrational irritability and anger.

Biblical examples: Jonah (Jonah 4:4, 9); Moses (Num. 20:10–11).

Do you feel your life is worthless?

It may be that your life is highly valued by others and that you are useful to others and to the Lord. But because of your distorted view of yourself, you feel your life is worthless. Indeed, you may feel your life is just a burden to and a blight upon others.

Biblical examples: Job (Job 3:3–26); Jeremiah (Jer. 20:14–18).

Do you feel extreme anxiety or panic?

The authors of *I'm Not Supposed to Feel Like This* explain what happens when a person is overwhelmed by anxiety: "In anxiety, the person often *overestimates* the threat or danger they are facing, and at the same time usually *underestimates* their own capacity to cope with the problem."[4] Panic attacks are really the rapid onset of extreme anxiety about some imagined catastrophic event. They last only fifteen to thirty minutes, but the person usually wants to flee the situation.

Biblical examples: David (1 Sam. 21:12); disciples (Matt. 8:25).

Do you feel God hates you and is far from you?

Although to any outside observer your past and your present may be replete with examples of God's good

---

4. Chris Williams, Paul Richards, and Ingrid Whitton (London: Hodder & Stoughton, 2002), 31.

favor toward you, you feel that God has either become your enemy or else has given up on you. You feel as if you are in spiritual darkness. The Bible is a "dead" book to you, and prayer is almost impossible.

Biblical examples: Job (Job 6:4; 13:24; 16:11; 19:11; 30:19–23, 26); Jeremiah (Lam. 3:1–3).

Do you feel suicidal or do you have a longing to die? These deeply depressed feelings are movingly articulated for us by Charles Spurgeon, as he commented on the experience of Heman in Psalm 88:

> He felt as if he must die. Indeed he felt himself half dead already. All his life was going, his spiritual life declined, his mental life decayed, his bodily life flickered; he was nearer dead than alive. Some of us can enter into this experience for many a time have we traversed this valley of death shade, and dwelt in it by the month together. Really to die and to be with Christ will be a gala day's enjoyment compared with our misery when a worse than physical death has cast its dreadful shadow over us. Death would be welcome as a relief by those whose depressed spirits make their existence a living death. Are good men ever permitted to suffer thus? Indeed they are; and some of them are even all their lifetime subject to bondage.... It is a sad case when our only hope lies in the direction of death, our only liberty of spirit amid the congenial horrors of

corruption.… He felt as if he were utterly forgotten as those whose carcasses are left to rot on the battlefield. As when a soldier, mortally wounded, bleeds unheeded amid the heaps of slain, and remains to his last expiring groan, unpitied and unsuccoured, so did Heman sigh out his soul in loneliest sorrow, feeling as if even God Himself had quite forgotten him. How low the spirits of good and brave man will sometimes sink. Under the influence of certain disorders everything will wear a somber aspect, and the heart will dive into the profoundest deeps of misery.[5]

Biblical examples: Job (Job 3:20–22; 6:9; 7:15–16); Moses (Num. 11:14); Elijah (1 Kings 19:4).

Bodily Symptoms

The Bible confirms for us the link between distorted thoughts or emotions and many of our bodily ailments: "A merry heart doeth good like a medicine: but a broken spirit drieth the bones" (Prov. 17:22). Every day, doctors are faced with patients complaining of various physical symptoms whose root problems are their depressed thoughts and feelings.

These bodily symptoms include disturbed sleep (Job 7:4, 13–15); tiredness (Pss. 6:6, 69:3); weight fluctuations (Job 17:7; 19:20); digestive problems (Lam.

---

5. "Psalm 88" in *Treasury of David*, 6 vols. (Grand Rapids: Zondervan, 1950), 4:3.

3:15); loss of appetite (Pss. 42:3; 102:4); bodily pain (Pss. 31:10; 32:3–4; 38:3); choking feelings and breathlessness (Psalm 69:1–2). In Psalm 32:3–4 the psalmist describes the bodily consequences of true guilt, but the same can also be the result of false guilt.

Behavior and Activity

As we might expect, the impact of depression on our thoughts, feelings, and bodies will inevitably have an effect on our behavior and activity. This is usually seen in two ways. First, we may stop doing things we enjoyed or that we were good at or that were good for us. This may involve no longer going to church or fellowships, not contacting family and friends, or the cessation of hobbies and other beneficial leisure interests. Second, we may start doing things that make us feel worse, like staying indoors, drinking alcohol, or pushing away people who care.

Summary

1. Assess the five areas of your life as outlined, perhaps with the help of a trained pastor, medical professional, or caregiver, and try to make an honest judgment about yourself. Remember that even one false thought pattern will have an adverse effect on your feelings, physical health, and activity patterns.

2. Try to remain open to the possibility that physical symptoms may well be related to depressed thoughts and feelings.

3. If serious symptoms persist for a few weeks and nothing seems to be helping, seek medical advice regarding the suitability of antidepressants for you.

4. Focus particularly on the area of your thoughts and try, with God's help, to reverse false thinking patterns and recover and maintain a true view of God, of yourself, and of others. Take your time and focus on one area at a time.

5. Pray for yourself and others. Tell the Lord exactly how you feel. Job, David, Elijah, and Jeremiah did not hide their feelings from God.

6. Seek the sympathy of Christ. The words used to describe his mental sufferings in Matthew 26:37 and Mark 14:33 may be translated "surrounded with sadness" or "deeply depressed." Charles Spurgeon wrote:

> When our Lord bore in His own person the terrible curse which was due sin, He was so cast down as to be like a prisoner in a deep, dark, fearful dungeon, amid whose horrible glooms the captive heard a noise as of rushing torrents, while overhead resounded the tramp of furious foes. Our Lord in His anguish was like a captive in the dungeons, forgotten of all mankind, immured amid horror, darkness, and desolation.[6]

7. Believe the depression is part of the "all things" that are working together for your good (Rom. 8:28). John Lockley writes:

> If [God] had said, "Go out and preach....", you'd have gone. If He'd said, "I want you to be a missionary," you'd have gone (possibly reluctantly, depending upon your own hopes and desires!). But because He has said, "Sit there and be depressed for a bit, it will teach you some important lessons,"

6. "Psalm 40" in *Treasury of David*, 6 vols. (Grand Rapids: Zondervan, 1950), 2.235.

you don't feel that it is God calling you at all...*do you?*

Do you remember Naaman, who wanted to be cured of his leprosy? (See 2 Kings 5.) If he had been asked to do something glorious he would have been happy. Because he was asked to bathe in the murky old Jordan he wasn't so keen—yet this was God's plan for him, and it cured him. God has better plans for us than we have for ourselves—unfortunately, as we can't see into the future, we don't always appreciate just *why* God's plans are better. With hindsight it's somewhat easier!

However strange it may seem to you, *God wants you to go through this depression*—so look at it positively, not negatively. What does He want you to learn from it? What can you gain from going through it?

When you begin to think in this fashion your guilt feelings start to drop away. You can begin to understand that what is happening is part of God's plan for you—and *so your depression is not a punishment from God.* You are actually where God wants you to be, even if it is emotionally painful. To put it another way, if God wants you to go through this it would be wrong for you to avoid it, wouldn't it?[7]

7. *Practical Workbook for the Depressed Christian* (Bucks: Authentic Media, 2002), 18.

4 | THE CAUSES

In previous chapters I mentioned some of the causes of depression. I also noted the complexity of trying to analyze the causes of depression and concluded that it is often a combination of various factors. In this chapter we will look in more detail at the various causes of depression, and in the following chapter we will consider some of the cures for depression.

Depression is often divided into two main categories—reactive and endogenous. Reactive depression is usually traced to some obvious trigger, perhaps a stressful life event or unhelpful thought patterns. Endogenous depressions are thought to be organic or biological in origin. It is the name usually given to depressions that seem to have no obvious external trigger, and they are often traced to genetic predisposition. However, this distinction between reactive and endogenous is not as clear cut as it was once thought to be, as skilled investigation of many so-called endogenous depressions will often reveal a "trigger event," though a genetic predisposition may mean that the trigger is relatively small. We will consider five triggers of depression: stress, psychology, sin, sickness, and sovereignty.

Stress

When you stretch a piece of elastic, you can often extend it to two or even three times its size. However, the further you stretch it, the greater the tension on the rubber, the less flexible it becomes, and the greater the danger of its eventually snapping. Like rubber bands, we are all "stretched" from time to time. We are stretched by life events, which we have little control over, and by our lifestyle, over which we do have considerable control. Let's look at these two stretching forces.

Life events

Life events include marriage, relocating, exams, bereavement, illness, unemployment, and birth of children. Each of these events puts a strain upon us to one degree or another. When we are "stretched" in this way, our body and brain chemistry changes, and one of the results is often a dip in, or lowering of, our mood. This is normal. And, as the stressful events pass, our body and brain chemistry usually returns to normal along with our mood.

Sometimes, however, these stressful experiences can continue over a lengthy period, or they can occur one on top of another, or they can affect us more seriously than other people. The result is that our body and brain chemistry remains abnormal, as does our mood. We just can't pick ourselves up, no matter how many people urge us to. This is depression. At the very worst, like an elastic band, we can "snap," sometimes unexpectedly. This is what some call a nervous breakdown.

Changes in body chemistry, especially brain chemistry, greatly affect our ability to think and feel in a balanced way. Stressful events make our minds go into overdrive, exhausting and depleting the chemicals we need to think and feel in a normal and helpful way. Think of a computer with too many programs open and working at the same time and how this slows down all the processes until eventually the machine "crashes."

Lifestyle

While we have little if any control over life events, we do have substantial control over our lifestyle— the proportion of time and energy we give to work, socializing, shopping, traveling, recreation, exercise, rest, and sleep. Much of the increase in depression and anxiety today is largely the result of an unbalanced lifestyle where people are, on the one hand, working too hard and spending too much and, on the other hand, are exercising, resting, and sleeping too little. This deliberate stretch beyond our capacities and abilities is not glorifying God in our body and spirit (1 Cor. 6:20). It is also a breach of the sixth commandment, which requires us to take "all lawful endeavors to preserve our own life" (Westminster Shorter Catechism 68). The effects and result of a stressful lifestyle will often be the same as that of stressful life events—depression.

Psychology (The Way We Think)

In chapter 3 we looked at ten false thought patterns that contribute to depression. It is vital to learn to recognize these unhelpful thoughts by prayerful self-examination. It is also important and useful to note that some of these habits of thinking may be involuntarily absorbed or learned in early life from our parents and have become deeply ingrained. The authors of *I'm Not Supposed to Feel Like This* explain it this way:

> One consequence of the Fall is that we are brought up in a world that has been damaged, and our own experience of being brought up is likely to have damaged us in at least some ways. No matter how loving our parents have been, they will not always have reacted in the ways that we really needed. For some of us, our experience with our parents will have been largely a good one, for others it may have been very bad. Whatever your own experiences, it is likely that as you grew up you learned a range of helpful and unhelpful rules about how you see and judge

yourself, other people and the world around you. It is in childhood that these central ways of seeing things are first learned from your relationship with important people such as parents, brothers or sisters. In these relationships you should have received love, consistency and support, but sometimes the opposite occurs—rejection and inconsistency—and this can undermine us as we grow up. These central ways of seeing things are called core beliefs. Common core beliefs may be based around positive themes such as seeing yourself as good or successful at something, or more negative themes such as being a failure, bad, worthless, unlovable, incompetent, foolish or weak. Most people develop a range of both positive and negative core beliefs during their childhood and these can stay with us into our adult lives.[1]

When we feel down or when we are stressed, these core beliefs, these latent false thinking patterns, tend to occur more frequently and dominate. This can often lead to depression, worsen an existing depression, and, if persisted in, make recovery from depression much harder. Sometimes the church can reinforce or add to false thinking patterns by focusing on the things that the Bible forbids and how far short people's lives fall from biblical standards, and this may discourage

---

1. C. Williams, P. Richards, I. Whitton (London: Hodder & Stoughton, 2002), 15.

or depress people, especially when they aren't consistently assured of Christ's forgiveness and grace.

Sin

Non-Christians may be depressed because of their sin, in which case the cure is repentance and faith in Jesus Christ. Sadly, many depressed unbelievers are being treated with chemicals when what they need is conversion. If you are unconverted and depressed, then seriously consider whether your depression is related to a guilty conscience and conviction of sin. If so, then what you need is repentance from sin and faith in Jesus Christ. There are many Christians who will testify that this was the key to relieving their depression.

While sin may be the last thing unconverted people may think is causing their depression, the opposite is true for Christians. When a Christian becomes depressed, there are often painful spiritual consequences, such as a loss of assurance. Depressed believers then jump to the conclusion that there is also a spiritual cause—usually their own sins or hypocrisy or failures of one kind or another. However, just as it is usually wrong to think that there is a spiritual cause for cancer, it is also wrong to think of depression this way. As for non-Christians, depression in the Christian is often caused by stressful life events and lifestyles or unhelpful thought patterns, which I have already described in this chapter. Here are some sample quotations from various experienced Christian pastors, psychiatrists, counselors, and doctors on this point:

> True spiritual causes of depression are not common. Most Christians with an apparently religious content to their depression in fact have one of the mental/emotional causes rather than a true spiritual cause. *I cannot emphasise enough that solely spiritual causes of depression are infrequent in Christians.*[2]

> David and other psalmists often found themselves deeply depressed for various reasons. They did not, however, apologize for what they were feeling, nor did they confess it as sin. It was a legitimate part of their relationship with God. They interacted with Him through the context of their depression.[3]

We completely agree that there are always spiritual aspects to anxiety and depression (as there are in everything in life for a Christian). However, we see these as being a secondary consequence of the emotional distress that is part of these illnesses. Strong claims that all anxiety and depression is spiritual in origin are unhelpful because they

---

2. John Lockley, *A Practical Workbook for the Depressed Christian* (Bucks: Authentic Media, 1991), 58.

3. Steve and Robyn Bloem, *Broken Minds* (Grand Rapids: Kregel, 2005), 204.

miss the point that the actual problem is anxiety and depression.[4]

I would not go quite so far as John Lockley in saying that "True spiritual causes of depression are not common." However, I agree with the instinct to oppose the common position that depression is always caused by personal sin. I emphasize this point again and again, because blaming our depression on our sin is not only often wrong, it is also harmful. It is harmful because it increases false guilt and deepens feelings of failure. It also makes depressed Christians seek a spiritual solution to a problem that may actually originate in the body, life events, lifestyle, or unhelpful thought patterns.

However, having said all that, we must still leave open the possibility that a depression may sometimes be the result of specific sin or sins (as David describes in Ps. 32). The Westminster Confession of Faith says: "The most wise, righteous, and gracious God doth oftentimes leave, for a season, His own children to manifold temptations, and the corruption of their own hearts, *to chastise them for their former sins . . .*" (WCF 5.5, emphasis added).

How, then, does a Christian know if his depression has a spiritual cause or simply spiritual consequences?

---

4. Chris Williams, Paul Richards, and Ingrid Whitton, *I'm Not Supposed to Feel Like This* (London: Hodder & Stoughton, 2002), 121.

A *Practical Workbook for the Depressed Christian* puts it like this:

> For the Christian, *truly spiritual* causes of depression usually involve behaviour which the Christian knows to be wrong, but which he still deliberately and arrogantly persists in…. I am *not* talking about repeated sins that the Christian wishes he could control but can't…but *a deliberate and continued rebellion against God.*[5]

Ed Welch makes some more detailed and searching suggestions. He asks:

Do you see any of these things in your life?

- If you made someone besides God the center of your life, and you lose him or her, you will feel isolated and without purpose. Can you see how this can give way to depression? You made another person your reason for living and now, without him or her, you feel hopeless and unable to go on. You may not realize it, but the Bible tells us that this is idol worship—you are worshipping what God created instead of him.

- If you feel like you failed in the eyes of other people, and your success and the opinions of others is of critical importance, you can slip

---

5. Lockley, 57.

into depression. Can you see the spiritual roots? Your success and the opinions of others have become your gods, they are more important to you than serving Christ.

- If you feel like you did something very wrong, and you want to manage your sin apart from the cross of Jesus, depression is inevitable. We always want to believe that we can do something—like feeling really bad for our sins—but that is just pride. We actually think that we can pay God back, but this attitude minimizes the beauty of the cross and Jesus' full payment for sin.

- If you are angry and don't practice forgiveness, you can easily slide into depression. The simple formula is sadness + anger = depression. What makes us angry shows us what we love and what rights we hold dear. Unforgiveness shows us that we are not willing to trust God to bind up our broken hearts and to judge justly. Deal with your sadness and anger by pouring your heart out to God. Use the psalms as your prayers. Ask for faith so that you can trust God to be your defender and your helper."[6]

---

6. "Hope for the Depressed," *Restoring Christ to Counseling and Counseling to the Church (CCEF),* http://www.ccef.org/print/684?page=2 (accessed May 28, 2010).

Sickness

Thankfully, some in the biblical counseling movement have come to accept some role for medication in the treatment of some depressions. However, as they are usually focused on heart issues being the root cause, they usually minimize its role, often describing it in terms of merely "symptom alleviation." Implicitly and explicitly they suggest that there are always underlying issues, variously described as issues of meaning or relationship, what you are living for and how you are living, or the two great commandments. In other words, the default position in dealing with depressed people is that personal sin has caused their depression and they are responsible for it, so they must repent and believe the gospel. Of course, as I have said, personal sin can and often does cause (or contribute to) depression and anxiety, just as personal sin can and often does cause (or contribute to) heart disease or certain types of diabetes or even blindness. But these same diseases and disabilities can also be the result, not of personal sin, but of living in a fallen body in a fallen world. They can be the result of simple bodily sickness.

Just as the curse on this world and our bodies can cause mechanical, chemical, and electrical problems in our hearts, our livers, our pancreas, our eyes, and other body parts, so we can also have mechanical, chemical, and electrical problems in our brains, which may affect the way we think, and even our personalities. Many of us have seen friends or loved ones with brain injuries, bleeds, or tumors undergo distressing personality changes. Nutritionists have demonstrated how certain foods can affect our moods and thoughts, our feeling and thinking. Emotions can also be affected by exhaustion, diabetic hypos, exercise, hormonal changes, gland disorders, high blood pressure, and even sunshine.

As the brain is the most complex organ in our body, it is liable to be the most affected of all our organs by the Fall and the divine curse on our bodies. And as processing our thoughts is the main activity of our brain, we can expect this area at times to fail and break, through no fault of our own, with subsequent emotional and behavioral problems. That isn't to deny that a person is responsible for how he responds to mechanical, chemical, or electrical failures and faults in any part of his body.

In these cases, medication is not merely alleviating symptoms, but addressing the causes of depression— its physical causes. Treating a depressed person with medication is often no different from my giving my eight-year-old daughter one of her many daily injections of insulin for diabetes. I am not merely alleviating symptoms, but addressing the cause—depleted insulin due to dying or dead cells in her pancreas. And if she is lethargic, weepy, or irrational due to low sugar levels, I do not ask her what commandments she has broken or what "issues of meaning and relationship" she has in her life. I pity her, weep for her, and thank God for His gracious provision of medicine for her.

If we come to the point that our default position in dealing with the causes of depression is that it is sin until proven otherwise, we are getting painfully close to the disciples' position: "Master, who did sin, this man, or his parents?" (John 9:2). It is also a position that is somewhat akin to the health, wealth, and prosperity gospel, in which the diagnosis for trials is personal sin and the prescription is more repentance and faith.

I was a pastor for twelve years on the west coast of the Scottish Highlands. Sadly, that beautiful area has one of the highest rates of depression in the Western world, and I dealt with many Christians who endured years of mental suffering and spiritual darkness. Although initially, in my youthful zeal, I probed for the underlying "sin" or "issues" because I did not want just to "alleviate symptoms," I came to realize that I was often (though not always) dealing with people whose problem was not "issues of meaning or relationship." As I got to know them, I came to see that what they were living for and how they were living was not the problem; they were unquestionably living for and like Christ. In fact, they were among the godliest Christians I have ever met. The Lord was everything to them, and they would not let go of Him despite everything screaming from within and without, "There is no God!" Their problem was a sick brain, often suffering from the effects of long winter months with limited daylight hours.

So I would encourage pastors dealing with depressed people to fight strongly against adopting these immediate assumptions about the causes of depression: "It's sin until proven otherwise"; "There are always issues, underlying issues"; "It's about what she is living for and how she is living"; or "It's about the two great commandments." It may well be. But let's not begin there and potentially damage some of the precious people of God in their moments of greatest weakness.

Sovereignty

One final cause of depression in the Christian is the sovereignty of God. Hard though it may be to accept, the ultimate cause may be, "It pleased God." This, however, is not some sheer arbitrary, sadistic, and pointless infliction of suffering. Not at all. God has wise and loving motives and purposes in all His dealings with His children. The Westminster Confession of Faith says that God will sometimes allow His children to descend into the depths of depression "to discover unto them the hidden strength of corruption and deceitfulness of their hearts, that they may be humbled; and to raise them to a more close and constant dependence for their support upon Himself, and to make them more watchful against all future occasions of sin, *and for sundry other just and holy ends*" (WCF 5.5, emphasis added).

A well-known example of this is Job, where God allowed Satan to afflict His beloved servant. A lesser-known example is Hezekiah. "God left him, to try him, that he might know all that was in his heart" (2 Chron. 32:31). This does not mean that God actually left Hezekiah. God will never leave nor forsake His people. This is not an objective leaving, but a subjective leaving. God withdrew Himself from Hezekiah's spiritual feelings so that he lost his sense of God's presence, protection, and favor. So Hezekiah felt like God had left him. But God had a wise and loving purpose in this. It was to test Hezekiah and to reveal to him what was in his heart when God's felt presence was withdrawn.

Sometimes we take God's presence in our lives for granted. We forget what we might be without Him. He may wisely, temporarily, and proportionately withdraw the sense of His favor and presence to remind us of our state without Him and to lead us to greater thankfulness and appreciation for Him. He may do this by acting directly on our feelings. But He may also produce the same effects by lovingly afflicting our brain, disrupting its chemistry and electricity, just as He does when He lovingly afflicts one of His dear children with epilepsy, or any other disease.

Let me close this chapter with a quotation from Martyn Lloyd-Jones, a physician of the body who became a physician of the soul:

Now we turn to consider the "wiles of the devil" as they are to be seen in the confusion he creates between the physical, the psychological and the spiritual realms.... The subject is one of the most practical we can ever consider. We are strange creatures, made up of body, mind, and spirit; these are interrelated and react upon one another. Many of our troubles in life are due to this fact, and to our failure to realize the place, function, and sphere of each one of these realms.[7]

---

7. *The Christian Warfare* (Grand Rapids: Baker, 1976), 206–208.

5 | THE CURES

In the last chapter we looked at some of the causes of depression. Now we will look at some of the cures. However, before we do so, we must ask the depressed person a vital question: "Do you want to be made whole?" This was the question Jesus asked of the lame man at the pool of Bethesda (John 5:6). At first glance it may seem like a silly question. Surely every sick person wants to be made whole! Surely everyone with problems wants them solved! However, Christ's question may imply that the man was not making use of all the means available to get better. Or, perhaps he had given up hope of getting better. These are common scenarios with depression. Doctors and pastors are often faced with the frustrating situation of people who need the help they can give, yet are not taking the steps required to benefit from this help. Perhaps they have just learned to live with the problem. Perhaps they have given up hope of getting better. Perhaps they lack the will to play their part in the healing process. Perhaps they are frightened of all the responsibilities of life that would come upon them should they be viewed as well again. Perhaps they would miss the attention and sympathy that being ill may generate. These are all possibilities. So, if you are depressed, the first searching question you must ask yourself is, "Do I want to be made whole?" You have no hope of recovery from depression unless you want to recover and are, therefore, prepared to play your own significant part in the recovery process.

We will look at four measures that should be considered parts of a "package" of healing.

Correct Your Lifestyle

It is vital to lead a balanced lifestyle in order to relieve the "stretch" that threatens our physical, mental, emotional, and spiritual well-being. Some of these practical points also apply to depressions resulting from stressful life events.

Routine

One of the keys to a balanced lifestyle is regular routine. This is also one of the first things to fall by the wayside when someone becomes depressed. Depressed people often find it difficult to resist being guided by their feelings. When a person feels down he will often do only what he feels like doing and avoid what he doesn't feel like doing. For example, if you are depressed and you don't feel like getting up, you won't. If you don't feel like working, you won't. If you don't feel like doing the laundry, you won't. If you feel you want to drink or eat to excess, you do it. A positive step in recovering from depression is to restore order and discipline in your life. Regular and orderly sleeping, eating, and working patterns will rebuild a sense of usefulness and healthy self-esteem. It is also glorifying to God who is a God of order, not of confusion (1 Cor. 14:33).

Relaxation

We need to build times of relaxation into our lives. This may involve finding a quiet spot at various times throughout the day to simply pause, calm down, and seek the peace of God in our lives. Jesus recognized and provided for this need in His disciples when He took them "apart into a desert place, and rest[ed] a while" (Mark 6:31).

Another helpful area to explore is whether you are breathing properly. It is common for depressed and especially for anxious people to be extremely tense, which often leads to hyperventilation or over-breathing and then to inevitable weakness of body and brain. There are many helpful books and Web sites that, without straying into "New Age" ideas, give good basic advice on re-learning how to relax and breathe properly.

Recreation

Moderate physical exercise helps to expel unhelpful chemicals from our system and stimulates the production of helpful chemicals. Outdoor exercise has the added benefit of the sun's healing rays.

Rest

A Christian psychologist recently said to me that he starts most depressed people on three pills: "Good exercise, good diet, and good sleep!" That's great advice, so I would encourage you to make use of the plentiful resources available today on these subjects.

As regular sleep patterns enable the body and mind to repair and re-charge, set fixed times for going to bed and getting up, and try to get at least eight hours of sleep. Avoid caffeine, vigorous exercise, phone calls, TV, and Internet use within three hours of sleeping. Get into a set routine for going to bed, and try to secure cooperation from others in the house.

And remember God's gift of weekly rest. The Lord's Day was graciously made for us (Mark 2:27), partly to ease the tension of our busy, overstretched lives.

Reprioritize

Examine your life and see what you can do to reduce your commitments and obligations. Areas to consider are your family, your work, your church, your neighbors, and travel. Once you are better you may be able to pick up some of these activities again. But the priority is to get better.

Correct Your False Thoughts

As we have noted throughout these pages, one of the most common contributory factors to depression is wrong and unhelpful thoughts. Many Christians who wouldn't think of viewing God's Word in a false way still make the mistake of viewing God's world in a false way. As they view themselves, their situations, and their relationships with others, they tend to dwell on and magnify the negatives and exclude the positives. This distorted view of reality inevitably depresses their mood.

Christians are obliged to challenge falsehood and distortions of reality, especially when they find them in themselves. At the end of this chapter you will find a questionnaire to help you do this. The first part is to help you identify and examine your thoughts, and the second is to help you challenge your false and unhelpful thoughts. Questionnaires such as these are recommended for use by many Christian and non-Christian psychiatrists. They may look a bit strange to you, and you may wonder, "Isn't all this just psychological mumbo-jumbo?" However, I would like to show you here how each step is grounded in biblical Christian experience. Psalm 77 is a perfect example of Asaph's investigating and challenging his thoughts, with God's help, in order to raise his mood and spirits. There are also slightly more abbreviated versions of the same biblical strategy in Job 19, Psalm 42,

Psalm 73, and Habakkuk 3. So this is not "psychological mumbo-jumbo," but true Bible-based Christian experience. Let's look at Psalm 77 to prove this.

Asaph examines his thoughts

1. My life situation *Time? Place? People?* *Events?*	Asaph's life situation is not defined in detail in Psalm 77. Asaph calls it "the day of my trouble" (v. 2), a deliberately general description which fits many life situations.
2. My feelings *Sum up your mood* *in one word if you can.* *Are you sad, worried,* *guilty, angry, ashamed,* *irritated, scared, disap-* *pointed, humiliated,* *insecure, anxious?* *You may want to rate* *the intensity of your* *feeling by determining* *what percentage of* *the time you feel* *that way.*	Troubled (vv. 2, 3, 4) [100%] Inconsolable (v. 2) [90%] Overwhelmed (v. 3) [90%] Cut off from God (v. 7) [90%] Pessimistic (v. 7) [95%] Insecure (v. 2) [80%] Scared (v. 2) [75%]

3. My thoughts *What am I thinking of at this time? About myself? Others? The present? The future?*	My past was all great, but the present is all terrible (v. 5). God has cast me off (v. 7). The future is bleak and gloomy (v. 7). God's promises no longer hold true (v. 8). God has forgotten how to be gracious (v. 9). God has shut up His mercies (v. 9).
4. My analysis *Identify false or unhelpful thinking patterns such as false extremes, false generalization, false filter, etc. (see chapter 3 for others).*	The psalmist confesses to wrong and unhelpful thinking when he looks at his thought patterns and says, "This is my infirmity" (v. 10). His "infirmity," or his distorted thinking, includes false extremes, false generalization, false mind reading (of God), false fortune telling, false feeling-based reasoning (see chapter 3).
5. My behavior *Impact of 1–4 on me and my relations with others. Stopped helpful activities? Started unhelpful activities? Reduced activity? Hyper-activity?*	Crying (v. 1) Complaining (v. 3) Cannot sleep (v. 4) Cannot speak to others (v. 4) Cannot pray to God (v. 4)

Asaph challenges his own thoughts

Sometimes simply identifying such false thoughts and their impact on us can itself be a major turning point. However, to complete the process, we should go on to formally challenge our own false thoughts.

6. My reasons *Why do I believe the thoughts I listed in step 3 are true? What evidence is there to support my conclusion?*	The psalmist is not explicit but does imply: This is how I feel. This is how things look to me.
7. My challenge *List evidence and reasons against the thoughts in step 3. Think of what God would point to, to show you that your thoughts are not completely true.*	God has dealt with His dear people similarly before (v. 10). God's powerful providence through the years (vv. 11–20). God sometimes leads His people through deep waters (v. 19). God sometimes shepherds His people through the wilderness (v. 20). God will lead His people to the Promised Land (v. 20).

8. My conclusion *Come to a balanced conclusion, which will also be truthful and helpful.*	Although I feel cast off and forgotten by God, He is redeeming me and leading me through the wilderness into the Promised Land. Unlike God's Word and works, my feelings are infirm —inaccurate and unreliable.
9. My new feelings *Copy some or all of the feelings from step 2 and rate them again.*	Asaph is not explicit, but from his words in verses 13–20 we may reasonably infer that Asaph now feels a degree of confidence, optimism, safety, and comfort. Troubled [30%] Inconsolable [20%] Overwhelmed [15%] Cut off from God [30%] Pessimistic [10%] Insecure [10%] Scared [20%]
10. My plan *How will I put the balanced conclusion into practice?*	I will think more about God than myself. I will think more about God's deeds in the past. I will believe God's unchanging power and grace. I will trust even when in the deep waters or in the wilderness.

Correct Your Brain Chemistry

If assessing your feelings and thoughts (steps 2 and 3) does not work or you can't even get started, then I would suggest that you seek out trained medical personnel for diagnosis and possibly prescription of appropriate medication. And please do not wait until things have gotten so bad that you "crash" to a halt. The farther you fall, the longer it will take to return. Even a low dose of anti-depressant is sometimes enough just to begin to restore depleted brain chemicals and pick up your mood sufficiently to enable you to begin to take the steps necessary to correct your lifestyle and thoughts. However, more serious depressions sometimes require medication for two to five years in order to permanently restore the brain's chemistry and processes.

If you go to your doctor, you may find it helpful to write out some of your symptoms, how you have tried to manage them, and also what you think may have caused them. Sometimes that initial visit can be rather emotional, and you may forget important facts. Make a list of the questions you want to ask, especially about medications. There are a number of myths and false ideas about antidepressants: "If I take antidepressants I won't be my true self.... There will be horrible side effects.... I might get addicted.... People will look down on me.... It will mean I am crazy." Your doctor should be able to refute these myths and reassure you. However, as mentioned, antidepressants should not be viewed as a cure-all. You will still need to work at changing false and unhelpful thinking and harmful behavior.

I return to the Puritans for evidence to support the view that we must be extremely careful not to dismiss non-spiritual causes of depression. Richard Baxter wrote:

> Make as full a discovery as you can, how much of the trouble of your mind doth arise from your melancholy and bodily distempers, and how much from discontenting afflictions in your worldly estate, or friends, or name and according to your discovery make use of the remedy.
>
> I put these two causes of trouble together in the beginning, because I will presently dismiss them and apply the rest of these directions only to those troubles that are raised from sins and wants in grace.
>
> For melancholy, I have by long experience found it to have so great and common a hand in the fears and troubles of mind that I meet not with one of many, that live in great troubles and fears for any long time together, but melancholy is the main seat of them: though they feel nothing in their body but all in their mind. I would have such persons make use of some able godly physician, and he will help them to discern how much of their trouble comes from melancholy. Where this is the cause, usually the party is fearful of almost everything; a word or a sudden

thought will disquiet them. Sometimes they are sad, and scarce know why: all comforts are of no continuance with them; but as soon as you have done comforting them, and they be never so well satisfied, yet the trouble returns in a few days or hours, as soon as the dark and troubled spirits return to their former force....

Now to those that find that melancholy is the cause of their troubles, I would give this advice: Expect not that rational, spiritual remedies, should suffice for this cure; for you may as well expect that a good sermon, or comfortable words, should cure the falling sickness or palsy, or a broken head, as to be a sufficient cure to your melancholy fears: for this is as real a bodily disease as the other.... But because it works on the spirits and fantasy [imagination], on which words of advice do also work, therefore such words of advice do also work. Therefore such words, and Scripture and reason may somewhat resist it, and may palliate or allay some of the effects at the present; but as soon as time hath worn off the force and effects of these reasons, the distemper returns.[1]

---

1. "The Right Method for a Settled Peace of Conscience and Spiritual Comfort" in *The Practical Works of Rev. Richard Baxter,* 4 vols. (London: George Virtue, 1838), 2:888.

Correct Your Spiritual Life

Correct the spiritual consequences

I have emphasized that depression in Christians is often caused by nonspiritual factors. However, there are spiritual consequences in all depressions. There are a number of steps a depressed Christian can take to help reverse at least some of the spiritual consequences. You may find Martyn Lloyd-Jones's book *Spiritual Depression* to be helpful in this regard, although at times Dr. Lloyd-Jones can be a bit sweeping and dogmatic in his generalizations.

Here are some practical things you can do to help address the spiritual consequences of depression.

1. Accept that being depressed is not necessarily a sin and indeed is compatible with Christianity. Many Bible characters and many of the greatest Christians passed through times of depression.

2. Try to understand that your loss of spiritual feelings is not the cause of your depression, but rather the depression has caused a general loss of feeling in all parts of your life, your spiritual life included.

3. Patiently wait for the corrections in your lifestyle, thinking, or brain chemistry to have an effect on your feelings as a whole, and your spiritual life will pick up at the same time also.

4. Have a set time for reading your Bible and praying. Depressed Christians may either give up reading and praying, or they may try to read and pray excessively in order to try and bring back their spiritual feelings. Both approaches are unhelpful. Instead, set aside a regular time each day to read and pray. If concentration is a problem, keep things short (5–10 minutes) until you feel better. Setting unrealistic spiritual goals will only deepen depression. The Puritan Richard Baxter advised those suffering from depression:

> Avoid your musings, and exercise not your thoughts now too deeply, nor too much. Long meditation is a duty to some, but not to you, no more than it is a man's duty to go to church that hath his leg broken, or his foot out of joint: he must rest and ease it till it be set again, and strengthened. You may live in the faith and fear of God, without setting yourself to deep, disturbing thoughts.[2]

5. Bring objective truth to mind (for example, the doctrine of justification or the atonement), especially positive verses that set forth God's love, mercy, and grace for sinners (for example, Rom. 8:1; 8:38–39; 1 John 1:9; 1 John 4:9–10). You may

---

2. "The Cure of Melancholy and Overmuch Sorrow," in *The Practical Works of Rev. Richard Baxter,* 4 vols. (London: George Virtue, 1838), 4.932.

want to write out a verse and carry it around with you. When negative thoughts overwhelm you, bring out the verse and meditate upon it.

6. When you pray, tell God exactly how you feel. Be totally honest. Ask God to help you with your doubts and fears and to restore to you the joy of salvation. Thank Him for loving you and being with you even though you do not feel His love or presence. Praying for others who suffer can also help to turn your thoughts away from yourself for a time.

7. Keep going to church and seek out the fellowship of one or two sympathetic Christians you can confide in, and ask them to pray with you and for you. Be careful about who you talk to. Sadly, some Christians cannot keep confidences, and others will have little understanding of or sympathy for your condition.

8. Remember God loves you as you are, not as you would like to be.

Correct the spiritual causes

Previously, I mentioned the possibility that a Christian's depression may be the result of some specific sin or sins. If, having examined your life, you find that there is a sin that you are deliberately and stubbornly persisting in or other sins that you have never really repented of, it is time to fall on your knees and seek

God's pardon for the sin and God's power over the sin. See Psalm 32 and Psalm 51 for examples of how to do this.

After reading this chapter, you may feel that there is so much to do, that the mountain is so high, that there is no point in even trying. Certainly one of the biggest mistakes you can make is to try too much at once. You will fail and be even more depressed. Instead, preferably with someone's help, sit down and make a list of areas where you know you need to change. Then pick one problem area and focus on it alone. It is best to choose a specific area with a measurable and realistic possibility of change. Consider all the possible solutions, weighing the pros and cons. Then, prepare a written step-by-step plan and carry it out one step at a time. Have both short-term and long-term targets. Review the outcome, make any necessary adjustments, and be encouraged by any progress you have made. In summary:

- Ask someone to help you and keep you accountable.
- Focus on one problem at a time.
- Decide on the best solution.
- Write out a step-by-step plan.
- Set realistic short-term and long-term targets.
- Review to correct and also to encourage.

Above all, pray for God's help and His blessing on the steps as you go.

Thought Investigation Questionnaire

1. My life situation *Time? Place? People?* *Events?*	
2. My feelings *Sum up your mood in* *one word if you can.* *Are you sad, worried,* *guilty, angry, ashamed,* *irritated, scared, disap-* *pointed, humiliated,* *insecure, anxious? You* *may want to rate the* *intensity of your feeling* *by determining what* *percentage of the time* *you feel that way.*	
3. My thoughts *What am I thinking* *of at this time? About* *myself? Others? The* *present? The future?*	

4. My analysis
Identify false or unhelp-
ful thinking patterns
such as false extremes,
false generalization, false
filter, etc. (see chapter 3
for others).

5. My behavior
Impact of 1–4 on me and
my relations with others.
Stopped helpful activi-
ties? Started unhelpful
activities? Reduced activ-
ity? Hyper-activity?

6. My reasons
Why do I believe the
thoughts I listed in step 3
are true? What evidence
is there to support my
conclusion?

7. My challenge
List evidence and reasons
against the thoughts in
step 3. Think of what
God would point to,
to show you that your
thoughts are not com-
pletely true.

6 | THE CAREGIVERS

We now come to the final area of our study: caregivers. For the purposes of this book, caregivers are the depressed Christian's family and friends and fellow Christians who will be involved to one degree or another in helping the sufferer get better. Usually these caregivers have no medical training, and often they have limited or incorrect knowledge of depression or anxiety. However, they have a critical role in helping a depressed person get better. Research has shown that mental health patients get better much quicker if they can confide in and get support from someone close to them.

This chapter, then, will consider ten areas for caregivers to consider when they are trying to help a depressed person get better.

Study

As Christians, we surely want to be the person to whom our loved ones turn in time of need. And when they do turn to us, we want to be able to help them and not hurt them further. It is imperative, therefore, that we learn about depression in order to avoid the common mistakes that laypeople often make when dealing with the depressed and in order to be of maximum benefit to those who are suffering. As I mentioned in the preface, this book is a simple introduction to depression, a kind of quick emergency guide. However I would like to recommend some resources for further study.

Along with studying how Jesus dealt with the ill, the weak, and the distressed, you might want to read some of the helpful books, written from a Christian perspective, that are now available. The following are listed in order of readability and usefulness:

- *I'm Not Supposed to Feel Like This* by Chris Williams, Paul Richards, and Ingrid Whitton
- *Overcoming Spiritual Depression* by Arie Elshout
- *Broken Minds* by Steve and Robyn Bloem
- *A Practical Workbook for the Depressed Christian* by Dr. John Lockley[1]

Another book, of course, is the well-known *Spiritual Depression* by Dr. Martyn Lloyd-Jones. However, you should be aware that in that book Dr. Lloyd-Jones does not deal with every aspect of depression as an illness but rather focuses on some of the spiritual

---

1. I strongly disagree with some of the material in chapter 19.

consequences of depression. In some ways, the book is more about spiritual discouragement than depression, but it is helpful nevertheless.

A book written from a non-Christian perspective, but which is still useful for changing unhelpful thought patterns and behavior, is *Mind over Mood* by Dennis Greenberger and Christine Padesky.

I would also cautiously recommend Ed Welch's *Blame It on the Brain?* and *Depression: A Stubborn Darkness.* Dr. Welch exhibits a sensitive balance when dealing with depression, and his books have a lot of excellent and helpful material. He seems to be open to non-spiritual causes of depression, although at times he still seems to revert to the "medicine only alleviates symptoms" model. *A Stubborn Darkness* is also helpful for exploring possible spiritual causes or contributors to depression. However, I would hesitate to put this book directly into the hands of depressed Christians, as they will often draw the worst possible conclusions about themselves, regardless of objective reality. It is better that a committed and understanding pastor or family member gently and wisely guide a depressed person through the relevant parts of the book.

It is important to remember that reading these books will not turn you into a mental health expert, but it will make you more useful and helpful to loved ones in distress. It will also help you to know your limitations so that you make the right decision about when to advise someone to see a more experienced

Christian, a doctor, or a mental health professional. I would recommend that pastors build a database of local doctors and mental health professionals who share their Christian principles. Phone around, speak to people, visit hospitals, speak to the staff, and build relationships so that when you are facing a situation that is beyond your competence, you will know to whom you should turn.

Sympathy

Thoughtful and prayerful study of depression should naturally and automatically increase our sympathy for those who suffer from it. By *sympathy*, I mean an ability to communicate that we truly understand the problem and the symptoms, that we are deeply concerned, and that we will do all that we can to help. In many cases such sympathy can have a powerful therapeutic effect on the sufferer. The lack of it can only multiply the pain and deepen the darkness. Consider the following quote from Russell Hampton, who suffered from depression:

> If there were a physical disease that manifested itself in some particularly ugly way, such as postulating sores or a sloughing off of the flesh accompanied by pain of an intense and chronic nature, readily visible to everyone, and if that disease affected fifteen million people in our country, and further, if there were virtually no help or succour for most of these persons, and

they were forced to walk among us in their obvious agony, we would rise up as one social body in sympathy and anger. There isn't such a physical disease, but there is such a disease of the mind, and about fifteen million people around us are suffering from it. But we have not risen in anger and sympathy, although they are walking among us in their pain and anguish.[2]

It will greatly help you to sympathize if you always remember that you could just as easily be in the same position, suffering the same sorrow (1 Cor. 4:7). If you treat depressed people with impatient contempt, you may, like many others before you, have to learn sympathy the hard way.

Support

Support follows sympathy. It involves being available to listen and talk either in person or at the end of a phone. It includes praying with the person, especially as the depressed person may find it impossible to put words and sentences together in prayer. It means unconditional love, love that is maintained even when you do not agree with every decision your loved one is making and even when that loved one may unjustly turn on you. It requires practical help such as babysitting to enable a young mother to get a few free hours

---

2. *The Far Side of Despair: A Personal Account of Depression* (Chicago: Nelson-Hall, 1975), 78.

each week or such as taking an elderly person out for a drive to give her a refreshing change of scenery. You will need wisdom to recognize when the help you are providing is not enough and the depressed person needs expert support from medical services. The benefits of such supportive friendship cannot be overestimated:

> The presence, the availability, just the existence of a friend like this provides a tremendous degree of comfort to the depressed person, as it demonstrates in physical terms how much he is cared for, accepted, loved, as he is, warts and all. It is not difficult for the depressed person to go on to realise that if individual Christians can love him that much, how much more will *God* do the same....
>
> Unconditional friendship is the key, as is loyalty. The real friends are the ones who can accept the depressed person as he is—on good days, bad days, sad days, frightened days and angry days. Friends like this don't put pressure on in any way, but allow the sufferer to be himself, however horrid that may seem to be. As one of my depressed friends said, "It's a relief not to have to put on a disguise."[3]

On a congregational level, pastors and office bearers should encourage a supportive atmosphere:

---

3. John Lockley, *A Practical Workbook for the Depressed Christian* (Bucks: Authentic Media, 2005), 338.

For our churches to be really effective in support-
ing those with mental health difficulties, we need
to establish a culture where everyone in the local
church knows that it is acceptable to have problems from time to time, and that the church as a
whole—and especially its leadership—is there to
support church members during these times as
well as in times of success.[4]

The church should be especially aware of the need
to support the supporters. To be an effective support
to the mentally ill is physically, mentally, emotionally, and spiritually demanding. As Christians we
need to be conscious of the need not only to support
depressed people but also to minister to the needs of
their nearest and dearest.

Stigma

There is still a stigma attached to mental illness and
to depression in particular. Ignorance and misunderstanding have filled the public mind with many
prejudices and falsehoods. As a result, many still view
disorders such as depression as a choice or as a sign of
weakness or as an excuse to opt out of life. Depressed
people may also share these mistaken beliefs, which
increases their sense of guilt and failure. Conse-

---

4. Chris Williams, Paul Richards, Ingrid Whitton, *I'm
Not Supposed to Feel Like This* (London: Hodder & Stoughton,
2002), 236.

quently, they will often be reluctant to admit what they are feeling, resulting in their going for many long months, or even years, without asking for help or seeking treatment.

People who follow the first three steps in this chapter will help to reduce this stigma. But the church can also help by making clear that Christians do not have to be problem free and by demonstrating that when people do experience problems, they will not be ignored or avoided.

Also, the preacher should present a balanced view of the Christian life, as represented in the Psalms, over a third of which deal with fear, anxiety, and despair. This is part and parcel of normal Christian experience in an abnormal world. We should remind ourselves again and again: "For who maketh thee to differ from another? and what hast thou that thou didst not receive? now if thou didst receive it, why dost thou glory, as if thou hadst not received it?" (1 Cor. 4:7). Or to put it another way: "almost anyone can experience mental health problems, given the wrong sequence of life experiences and stressors."[5]

Secrecy

Because of the stigma attached to mental illness, it often takes a huge amount of courage for someone to admit to depression, often due to the fear of what peo-

---

5. Ibid., 237.

ple will say. If someone, therefore, trusts you enough to confide in you, then you must maintain the strictest confidence. There must be no "sanctified" gossip: "I'm just telling you this so that you can pray about it." It is tragic that so many depressed Christians have to prolong their secret suffering because of a justified fear that no one can keep a secret in the church. The church is in desperate need of Christians who are known to have this simple talent—they keep confidences.

Self-Esteem

Deeply rooted self-doubt and self-criticism will often emerge and strengthen during a depression. Depressed people often feel useless and worthless. They have low self-esteem. What should we do to address this?

Some Christians are reluctant to give people any praise or encouragement because of the risk of making a person proud. However, it is safe to say that pride is one of the least risky vices for someone who is depressed. Pride results from having an overinflated view of oneself. Depression usually involves the opposite.

Other Christians misconstrue the doctrine of original sin and total depravity to mean that there is no kind of good in anyone and fail to say anything positive to the depressed person. However, without minimizing the wickedness of the human heart and without denying our inability to do anything pleasing to God apart from faith in Christ, we should feel free to encourage depressed people to have a more realistic view of themselves by highlighting their God-given gifts, their contributions to the lives of others, their usefulness in society, and, if they are Christians, their value to the church. For example, a depressed young mother may feel like a total failure in every area of her life because she doesn't have a perfect home or perfect children. We can help such a person see that she achieves a lot in a day, even though she might not manage to do everything she would like. We might remind her of all the meals she makes, clothes she washes and irons, and the shopping she manages, helping her see herself and her life in a more accurate and realistic light. Arie Elshout comments,

> It is wrong to pat ourselves on the back when something has been accomplished as a result of our initiative. It is equally wrong, however, to focus on what we have not accomplished. In 1 Corinthians 15:10 we have a clear example of humility accompanied with a healthy opinion of one's accomplishments: "But by the grace of God I am what I am: and his grace which was bestowed upon me was not in vain; but I labored more abundantly than they all: yet not I, but the grace of God which was with me." Paul knew very well that he daily offended in many things (James 3:2; cf. Rom. 7; Phil. 3:12), and yet he did not go so far as to cast out all his accomplishments. I do not believe that this is God's will. In contrast to sinful forms of self-confidence and

self-respect, there are also those that are good, necessary, and useful. Without a healthy sense of these, human beings cannot function well. We may pray for an appropriate sense of self-confidence and self-respect, clothed in true humility, and we must oppose everything that impedes a healthy development of these things (be it in ourselves or others) with the Word of God.[6]

Subjectivism

One of the most common tendencies for those with depression is to focus on feelings and to base beliefs and conclusions on these feelings. This is especially true of Christians. For example, they may feel forsaken and conclude they are forsaken. Also, in an effort to restore true feelings, there is the tendency to read Bible passages and books that address the feelings. But such a focus on the subjective tends only to make things worse.

We should encourage the depressed person to move away from the realm of the subjective and to instead think on the objective truths of Christianity, things that are true regardless of our feelings: justification, adoption, the atonement, the attributes of God, and heaven, for example.

---

6. *Overcoming Spiritual Depression* (Grand Rapids: Reformation Heritage Books, 2006), 32–33.

Speak

The general rule is to listen much and to speak little. The following is a helpful list of what not to say:

- Pull yourself together.
- But you've got nothing to be sad about.
- Don't get so emotional.
- Oh, you'll soon get over it.
- It's a sin to be depressed.
- Just believe the promises.
- Smile, it can't be that bad.
- Well, things could be worse.
- At least it's nothing serious.
- You should confess your sins.
- You are not still on medication, are you?[7]

The more you understand depression, the less likely it is that you will say hurtful and damaging things.

Suicide

If you suspect someone is considering suicide, then you should sensitively and wisely ask the person if he is thinking along these lines and if he has already made a plan. Don't be afraid that such questions will plant suicidal thoughts in the depressed person's

---

7. Some of these examples are extracted from Steve and Robin Bloem, *Broken Minds* (Grand Rapids: Kregel, 2005), 234.

mind. Rather, realize that by asking, you may allow the suicidal person to admit his plans and seek professional help. This is vital and urgent if he tells you that he has gotten to the stage of making a plan.

Pastor Steve Bloem gives a number of reasons he has, at times, used to convince himself not to commit suicide:

- It is a sin and would bring shame to Christ and His church.
- It would please the devil and would weaken greatly those who are trying to fight him.
- It would devastate family members and friends, and you may be responsible for them following your example if they come up against intense suffering.
- It may not work, and you could end up severely disabled but still trying to fight depression.
- It is true—our God is a refuge (Ps. 9:10).
- Help is available. If you push hard enough, someone can assist you to find the help you need.
- If you are unsaved, you will go to hell. This is not because of the act of suicide but because all who die apart from knowing Christ personally will face an eternity in a far worse situation than depression.
- If you are a Christian, then Jesus Christ is interceding for you that your faith will not fail.
- God will keep you until you reach a day when your pain will truly be over.[8]

---

8. *Broken Minds* (Grand Rapids: Kregel, 2005), 59–60.

Slow

It is important to realize that there are no easy answers and there are no quick fixes in dealing with depression. It usually takes many months, and in some cases even years, to recover. You should, therefore, take a long-term view and patiently wait for improvement. Don't get frustrated over lack of progress, and be aware that temporary relapses may occur. John Lockley counsels:

> Patience is essential, because, by the nature of illness, the depressed person is likely to go over the same ground time and again, needing the same reassurance that was given a day, a week or a month ago.[9]

In the meantime let us take our depressed Christian brethren continually before the throne of grace and plead, "Lord, he whom Thou lovest is sick."

In the course of these chapters we have been looking particularly at how depression affects Christians. In closing I would like to refer to something that I have touched upon—the way God will sometimes use depression to bring an unconverted person to the Savior. If you are unconverted and feeling depressed, an important part of the solution is repentance from your sins and faith in Christ. That is not to say that

---

9. *A Practical Workbook for the Depressed Christian* (Bucks: Authentic Media, 2005), 338.

you may not need medication and counseling as well. However, medication and counseling will be only a temporary solution if you do not seriously address your spiritual state before God. Pills might get you through this world, but they will not be available in hell, the place of ultimate torment, despair, and gnashing of teeth. "Believe on the Lord Jesus Christ, and thou shalt be saved" (Acts 16:31).

APPENDIX

ON THE SUFFICIENCY OF SCRIPTURE:
SALVATION, SANCTIFICATION, AND SPECTACLES

The Bible does not give specific or detailed guidance on every moral and spiritual dilemma and issue. If it did, instead of having one book we can carry with us, we would have a library of volumes that we could never read in a lifetime. Does that mean God has left us lacking something? Not at all. This is how the Westminster Confession puts it:

> The whole counsel of God, concerning all things necessary for his own glory, man's salvation, faith, and life, is either expressly set down in Scripture, or by good and necessary consequence may be deduced from Scripture.... Nevertheless, we acknowledge the inward illumination of the Spirit of God to be necessary for the saving understanding of such things as are revealed in the Word; and that there are some circumstances concerning the worship of God, and the government of the Church, common to human actions and societies, which are to be ordered by the light of nature and Christian prudence, according to

the general rules of the Word, which are always
to be observed.[1]

The Confession's summary of biblical teaching is
fivefold. First, in many situations we face, the Bible's
instruction is explicit and detailed. It is "expressly set
down in Scripture."

Second, when the Bible does not have a particular
verse for our specific situation, we arrive at the instruction by "good and necessary consequence." We must
reason, deduce, and apply from general principles.

Third, God has deposited secondary areas of
knowledge in the general consensus of the human
community, even affecting areas like the circum-
stances of worship and church government. The
Christian consults this and learns from it, but this
secondary knowledge always is subject to God's
Word. We often call this "sanctified common sense."
The Confession calls it "the light of nature."

Fourth, the Bible does not cover any subject exhaus-
tively. It covers all things "necessary for [God's] glory,
man's salvation, faith, and life." If all you had in the
world was the Bible, you would have enough—you have
what is necessary to be saved, to believe, and to live to
God's glory in the world. It tells us everything we need
to know, but it does not tell us everything there is to
know. That's true even in subjects like salvation and the

---

1. WCF 1.6.

attributes of God. The Bible does not give us exhaustive knowledge, but rather comprehensive knowledge, necessary knowledge, sufficient knowledge.

Fifth, "the inward illumination of the Spirit of God [is] necessary for the saving understanding of such things as are revealed in the Word." For a saving understanding of Scripture, we need more than Scripture; we need the Holy Spirit to enlighten us.

I'd like to take a closer look at the phrases "good and necessary consequence" and "the light of nature."

Good and Necessary Consequence

What this means is that while we may not find a specific verse about our problem or need, we will always find a principle or guideline that we can apply to our situation. However, rigorous thought and prayer are necessary. We must not just sit around waiting for a voice or a vision. We must read Scripture prayerfully, seek the relevant principles, and by "good and necessary consequence," not by leaps of logic and irrationality, apply them to our situation.

For example, take the question "Whom shall I marry?" The Bible does not tell any of us the specific answer to this. Instead, there are general principles for the Christian to follow. We must marry "only in the Lord." Christian patience must be exercised. Your husband or wife should be willing to accept the roles and responsibilities that Scripture outlines. Wise counsel from older Christians should be sought. By "good and necessary consequence," by prayerful reasoning with these principles, you can find the answer.

Another question many of us ask is "What job will I do?" Again, there are no specific answers to this question, but there are sufficient general principles that we must think through. Will the job allow the full use of the talents God has given me? Will it compromise my Christian witness? Will the hours help or hinder my service for the Lord? Will the job give me enough money to provide for my family and me? Will I be able to do good to others in this work? By prayerfully thinking over these biblical principles you can find the answer.

When we consider the matter of what we should wear, we find that the Bible's principles are be modest, don't be extravagant, distinguish between the sexes, and consider the impact on others.

What about the church? There is much the Bible explicitly tells us about order in the church. There is much we can work out or deduce by prayerfully reasoning with biblical principles. However, there are some things that God has not said anything about in His Word, either explicitly or implicitly. For example, the Bible does not give us plans for building churches. It does not tell us how many services to have or when to have them. It does not tell us how many psalms to sing, prayers to pray, chapters to read. It does not tell us how long services should be. We decide these things using sanctified common sense, always acting under the general rules of the Word (1 Cor. 14:40). This brings us to the second phrase, "the light of nature."

The Light of Nature

This is an area where I fear many sincere believers are going wrong. Overreacting to attacks on the sufficiency of Scripture, they are going to an unbiblical "extreme sufficiency" position, thereby denying themselves many of God's riches. The sufficiency of Scripture does not mean that we should shun every nonbiblical source of knowledge. As the confession makes clear, even in some areas of worship and church government we must learn from what the human community has found helpful and useful. John Piper put it like this:

> To be obedient in the sciences we need to read science and study nature. To be obedient in economics we need to read economics and observe the world of business. To be obedient in sports we need to know the rules of the game. To be obedient in marriage we need to know the personality of our spouse. To be obedient as a pilot we need to know how to fly a plane.
>
> The sufficiency of Scripture means we don't need any more special revelation. We don't need any more inspired, inerrant words. In the Bible God has given us, we have the perfect standard

for judging all other knowledge. All other knowledge stands under the judgment of the Bible.[2]

John Calvin used the illustration of spectacles to explain this.[3] He said that the Bible is not only what we read, but what we read with. We use its pages as spectacles to view and read the world and the knowledge, the light of nature, God has distributed throughout it. Calvin explains:

> The human mind, however much fallen and perverted from its original integrity, is still adorned and invested with admirable gifts from its Creator.... We will be careful...not to reject or condemn truth wherever it appears....
>
> If we regard the Spirit of God as the sole foundation of truth, we shall neither reject the truth itself, nor despise it wherever it shall appear, unless we wish to dishonor the Spirit of God. Shall we say that the philosophers were blind in their fine observation and artful description of nature?... No, we cannot read the writings of the ancients on these subjects without great admiration. But if the Lord has willed that we be helped in physics, dialectic, mathematics, and other like disciplines, by the work and ministry of

---

2. "Thoughts on the Sufficiency of Scripture," Desiring God, http://www.desiringgod.org/ResourceLibrary/TasteAndSee/By Date/2005/1282_Thoughts_on_the_Sufficiency_of_Scripture/ (accessed March 5, 2010).

3. *Institutes*, 1.6.1.

the ungodly, let us use this assistance. For if we neglect God's gift freely offered in these arts, we ought to suffer just punishment for our sloths.[4]

I called this appendix "Salvation, Sanctification, and Spectacles" because the truth regarding salvation is expressly set down in Scripture; the truth regarding sanctification is expressly set down or may be deduced from Scripture; and knowledge in this world must be checked by Scripture or read through the lens of Scripture. It is in these senses that we have "everything pertaining to life and godliness" (2 Peter 1:3). It is in these senses that all Scripture "is profitable for doctrine, for reproof, for correction, for instruction in righteousness: that the man of God may be perfect, thoroughly furnished unto all good works" (2 Tim. 3:16–17).

Take, for example, eating. The Bible has some explicit instruction on eating and some principles that we can deduce. But the Bible does not tell us all we need to know about eating. So we learn from nutritionists (even non-Christian nutritionists) about how to eat in ways that will improve our physical, mental, emotional, and spiritual well-being. We read this knowledge through the lens of the Bible. The Bible is sufficient to keep us from falling into error as we read this world.

---

4. *Institutes*, 2.2.15–16.

The same goes for time management. We are given some principles in the Bible about time, some of which are explicit and some of which are deduced. But we can be helped to redeem the time by reading modern books on time management and organization—again, never leaving our spectacles off but rather reading and checking this knowledge with the Bible.

We take a similar approach to counseling. Some problems are, of course, entirely spiritual in nature and can be solved only by the Bible. But often the problems we face in counseling are a mixture of the spiritual, mental, relational, social, financial, and physical. In some cases the Scriptures will be explicit. In others we can deduce helpful principles. But in some areas we need to use our Bible as spectacles to read and learn from the knowledge God has distributed and deposited in the world. If we refuse to do this, if we say that we must separate ourselves from all knowledge outside the Bible, there is the risk of inadvertently undermining the sufficiency of Scripture. It is effectively saying that the Bible is not sufficient to help us read this world and learn from it, so we must separate ourselves from it. I believe the Bible is sufficient to enable us to read science and separate the wheat from the chaff, to separate valid observations and conclusions from the false, and so make use of the knowledge that God, in His "common grace" or "providence" has made known in His creation.

Eric Johnson has compared the Bible to the counselor's map on the trail of life, which God the great cartographer of life has drawn up.

> It includes a description of some of the major features of the landscape of human nature (including the best trails—those that lead to the greatest glory for God and well-being for humans), that give us an idea about where we are, where we are to go and how best to get to the proper end of our journey. Like a typical map, it does not provide every detail of the landscape (e.g., every tree). Maps are meant to provide a summary representation of the landscape and offer the essential information (the major streams, levels of elevation and trails) needed to locate one's present position and to help one get to where one is supposed to go. But a map is a necessity for one who hopes to make some progress and cover some ground. The necessity of Scripture, then, in relation to psychology and soul care means, the Bible is essential for properly understanding human beings and properly addressing their psychospiritual problems.[5]

So the Bible tells us where we are and where to go and provides all the essential markers to get us there. But there are details along the way, which we read

---

5. *Foundations of Soul Care* (Downer's Grove, IL: InterVarsity, 2007), 176–177.

through the lens of Scripture, and which can benefit us on our journey, as long as we do not leave the scriptural path. We, therefore, plot our course in this world with the chart of Scripture in our hands and the compass of the Holy Spirit in our hearts.